# BELT AND ROAD ECONOMICS

# BELT AND ROAD ECONOMICS

Opportunities and Risks of
Transport Corridors

# CONTENTS

**TABLES**

**BOXES**

APPENDIXES

## Acknowledgments

This study has been written by Michele Ruta (Team Leader; Lead Economist, Macroeconomics, Trade & Investment), Matias Herrera Dappe (Senior Economist, Transport), Somik Lall (Lead Economist, Social, Urban, Rural, & Resilience), and Chunlin Zhang (Lead Private Sector Specialist, Finance, Competitiveness & Innovation), with Erik Churchill (Consultant, Macroeconomics, Trade & Investment), Cristina Constantinescu (Economist, Macroeconomics, Trade & Investment), Mathilde Lebrand (Economist, Transport), and Alen Mulabdic (Analyst, Macroeconomics, Trade & Investment).

The study is an output of a research program led by the Macroeconomics, Trade & Investment Global Practice in collaboration with three other global practices: Transport; Finance, Competitiveness & Innovation; and Social, Urban, Rural, & Resilience. Caroline Freund (Director, Macroeconomics, Trade & Investment) provided guidance and supervision.

The content draws on background papers and inputs produced by Luca Bandiera, Suprabha Baniya, Marcus Bartley Johns, Paulo Bastos, Julia Bird, Mauro Boffa, Cecilia Briceno-Garmendia, Masud Cader, Alexander Cantor, Maggie Chen, Julian Latimer Clarke, Cristina Constantinescu, Francois De Soyres, Ben Derudder, Tania Ghossein, David Gould, Puja Guha, Daniel Zerfu Gurara, Bernard Hoekman, Tim Kelly, Clay Kerswell, Priyanka Kher, Charles Kunaka, Somik Lall, Mathilde Lebrand, Chuanhao Lin, Clay Lin, Mingqing Liu, Xingjian Liu, Elizabeth Losos, Maryla Maliszewska, Sara Mason, Gerard McLinden, Vikram Menon, Seth Morgan, Alen Mulabdic, Siobhan Murray, Lydia Olander, Georgi Panterov, Alex Pfaff, Tristan Reed, Nadia Rocha, Michele Ruta, Shujie Shao, Anirudh Shingal, Dimitry Sivaev, Daria Taglioni, Hua Tan, Trang Thu Tran, Alexandr Trubetskoy, Vasileios Tsiropoulos, Dominique van der Mensbrugghe, Tony Venables, Christina Wiederer, and Douglas Zhihua Zeng.

All finalized papers, data, and blogs have been posted on the World Bank website created and maintained by Erin Scronce and are available at https://www.worldbank.org/en/topic/regional-integration/brief/belt-and-road-initiative.

The team would like to thank the following World Bank Group Vice Presidents for their guidance: Ceyla Pazarbasioglu, Makhtar Diop, Laura Tuck, Victoria Kwakwa, Cyril Muller, Penny Goldberg, Hans Peter Lankes, and the late Jan Walliser. The study also benefited from the comments of Lilia Burunciuc, Bert Hofman, Martin Raiser, Guangzhe Chen, Shantayanan Devarajan, Karin Kemper, Ede Ijjasz-Vasquez, Deborah L. Wetzel, Zoubida Allaoua, Franz R. Drees-Gross, Simeon Djankov, Sameh Wahba, Rabah Arezki, Asli Demirguc-Kunt, Marianne Fay, Vivien Foster, Bill Maloney, Andrew Mason, Martin Rama, Sudhir Shetty, Hans Timmer, Albert G. Zeufack, Chang Yong Rhee, Antonio Nucifora, and Binyam Reja.

Many colleagues, inside and outside the World Bank Group, provided useful suggestions at various stages: Paul Amos, Swee Ee Ang, Elmas Arisoy, Bernard Aritua, Erhan Artuc, Valerio Crispolti, Bekele Debele, Doerte Doemeland, David Dollar, Baher El-Hifnawi, Alvaro Espitia

Rueda, Michael Ferrantino, Kathryn Funk, Indermit Gill, Anabel González, Rakesh Gupta Nichanametla, Richard Martin Humphreys, Martha Lawrence, Daniel Lederman, Peter Leonard, Jean-Francois Marteau, Aaditya Mattoo, Antonio Nunez, Israel Osorio-Rodarte, Cordula Rastogi, Daniel Reyes, David Rosenblatt, Julie Rozenberg, Susan Shen, Michael Toman, and Nicolaus Von Der Goltz.

Joseph Rebello, Erin Scronce, and Alejandra Viveros provided guidance on communications strategy. Bruce Ross-Larson and a team at Communications Development Incorporated edited the report. The graphic concept, design, and layout were carried out by Guillermo Varela and Estudio Prado. The cover artwork was created by Sasha Trubetskoy.

The team also thanks Rashi Jain in Washington, D.C., and Shanshan Ye in Beijing for their assistance in preparing the missions that supported this report.

## *Note on scope and terminology*

China has presented the Belt and Road Initiative (BRI) as an open arrangement in which all countries are welcome to participate. However, an official list of participating countries does not yet exist. In the absence of an official list, the effects of the BRI transport corridors can be assessed from two vantage points. The first is a country's geographical location with respect to the six overland corridors of the Silk Road Economic Belt and the 21st Century Maritime Silk Road (BRI corridors) as defined by China. The second is whether a country is a BRI signatory with China. The two approaches lead to different lists.

Official data from China states that 125 countries had signed collaboration agreements with China as of March 2019. Many of these countries are not located along the BRI corridors—some of them, for example, are in Latin America or in noncoastal parts of Africa. And some countries situated along the BRI corridors have not signed collaboration agreements with China.

This study uses the geographical approach, including the 71 economies detailed in appendix A. Most but not all have signed collaboration agreements with China. For this study, they are referred to as "Belt and Road corridor economies," or "corridor economies."

The study looks at the Belt and Road Initiative as a whole and does not provide cost-benefit analysis for individual corridors or projects. Since it focuses on connectivity and economics, it does not analyze energy infrastructure issues or geopolitical considerations.

## Foreword

Since it was announced by President Xi Jinping in 2013, China's Belt and Road Initiative (BRI) has been marked by both optimism and anxiety.

Many who see new business and trading opportunities from the initiative have touted its benefits for growth and development. Others have urged caution, noting significant risks—that developing countries might not be able to service BRI-related debt, that they might be left with stranded infrastructure, and that local communities and the environment could be harmed.

Quantifying impacts for a project as vast as the BRI is a major challenge. This study uses empirical research and rigorous economic modeling to provide countries with an objective analysis of opportunities and risks of Belt and Road transport corridors. It provides recommendations to maximize the benefits and mitigate the risks.

The analysis shows that Belt and Road transport corridors have the potential to substantially improve trade, foreign investment, and living conditions for citizens in the initiative's participating countries—but only if China and corridor economies adopt deeper policy reforms that increase transparency, expand trade, improve debt sustainability, and mitigate environmental, social, and corruption risks.

Countries that lie along the Belt and Road corridors are ill-served by existing infrastructure—and by a variety of policy gaps. As a result, they undertrade by 30 percent and fall short of their potential FDI by 70 percent. BRI transport corridors will help in two critical ways—lowering travel times and increasing trade and investment. Along economic corridors, the study estimates that travel times will decline by up to 12 percent once completed. Travel times with the rest of the world are estimated to decrease by an average of 3 percent, showing that non-BRI countries and regions will benefit as well.

Trade will also increase sharply, if unevenly, for Belt and Road corridor economies. The study estimates that trade will grow from between 2.8 and 9.7 percent for corridor economies and between 1.7 and 6.2 percent for the world. Countries that have a comparative advantage in time-sensitive sectors, such as fresh fruits and vegetables, or that require time-sensitive inputs, like electronics, will be among the biggest winners. Importantly, low-income countries are expected to see a significant 7.6 percent increase in foreign direct investment due to the new transport links.

Expanded trade and investment will increase growth and incomes in most corridor economies. Real income gains could increase by up to 3.4 percent at the high end of the study's estimates, but these gains would largely differ across countries, possibly leading some to incur welfare losses because of the large costs of infrastructure. BRI transport projects could help lift 7.6 million people from extreme poverty (those earning less than $1.90 a day) and 32 million people from moderate poverty (those earning less than $3.20 a day).

But these potential gains come with considerable risks. About one-quarter of Belt and Road corridor economies already have high debt levels, and for a handful of these economies, the analysis shows that medium-term vulnerabilities could increase. Even for countries without high debt levels, the trade-offs of a BRI investment must be considered carefully. Projects should be consistent with national development priorities. The value of individual transportation projects depends on realizing others. Improving coordination and cooperation—not just between China and individual recipient countries, but also among all of the countries on BRI corridors—will help BRI investments reach their full potential.

Complementary policy reforms are essential for countries to unlock BRI benefits. Real incomes for BRI corridor economies could be two to four times larger if trade facilitation is improved and trade restrictions are reduced. In landlocked Uzbekistan, for example, average income gains from infrastructure improvements are estimated at less than 1 percent. However, when complementary measures reduce border times, income gains increase to 9 percent. Stronger labor mobility and adjustment policies would ensure that gains are more equally shared.

Building infrastructure is inherently risky. Mitigating these risks will require improvements in data reporting and transparency—especially around debt. It will require open government procurement and adherence to high social and environmental standards. In April 2019, at the second BRI Forum, an open and fruitful discussion began on how to mitigate the risks. Achieving the ambitions of the Belt and Road Initiative will require equally ambitious reforms from participating countries, including China.

Critics and advocates both tend to see what they want in the BRI. Objective economic analysis will help participating countries choose the kinds of investments and reforms that will best meet their development needs.

**Ceyla Pazarbasioglu**
*Vice President, Equitable Growth, Finance, and Institutions*

# OVERVIEW

Opportunities and
risks of Belt and Road
transport corridors

China proposed the Belt and Road Initiative (BRI) in 2013 to improve connectivity and cooperation on a transcontinental scale. The scope of the initiative is still being deliberated, but it involves two main components, each underpinned by significant infrastructure investments: the Silk Road Economic Belt (the "Belt") and the New Maritime Silk Road (the "Road") (figure 1).

The overland "Belt" links China to Central and South Asia and onward to Europe. The maritime "Road" links China to the nations of South East Asia, the Gulf countries, East and North Africa, and on to Europe. Six overland economic corridors have been identified: the China–Mongolia–Russia Economic Corridor, the New Eurasian Land Bridge, the China–Central Asia–West Asia Economic Corridor, the China–Indochina Peninsula Economic Corridor, the China–Pakistan Economic Corridor, and the Bangladesh–China–India–Myanmar Economic Corridor.[1]

**Figure 1:** The Silk Road Economic Belt and New Maritime Silk Road

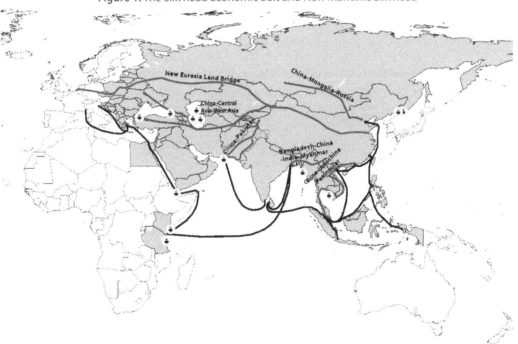

*Note:* Economies colored in blue are those along the BRI transport corridors. They have not necessarily signed collaboration agreements with China.

The goal of this study is to gather data that enables policymakers in more than 70 countries along these corridors to make evidence-based assessments of how to maximize the benefits and manage the risks of participating in the BRI.

---

[1] In the communique of the 2nd Belt and Road Forum in April 2019, the Bangladesh–China–India–Myanmar Economic Corridor is referred to as the China–Myanmar Economic Corridor.

- It provides evidence on how Belt and Road corridor economies could benefit from greater transport connectivity.

- It assesses the priorities and sequencing for policy reforms that could maximize the benefits of infrastructure investments

- It identifies the main risks and ways to manage them.

**The analysis shows that Belt and Road transport corridors could substantially improve trade, foreign investment, and living conditions for citizens in participating countries—but only if China and corridor economies adopt deeper policy reforms that increase transparency, expand trade, improve debt sustainability, and mitigate environmental, social, and corruption risks.**

Four main findings emerge from the analysis:

**1. Infrastructure and policy gaps in Belt and Road corridor economies hinder trade and foreign investment. New infrastructure can help close these gaps, but it is costly—and investments are occurring in the context of rising public debt.**

- *Trade in BRI corridor economies is estimated to be 30 percent below potential, and FDI is an estimated 70 percent below potential.* The economies accounted for close to 40 percent of global merchandise exports and 35 percent of foreign direct investment (FDI) inflows in 2017. Yet many corridor economies, particularly low-income countries, tend to be poorly integrated in regional and world markets—with low trade, small FDI inflows, and marginal participation in global value chains.

- *Trade and investment policies are often restrictive, and trade agreements between corridor economies tend to be shallow and fragmented.* Gaps in infrastructure compound gaps in policy, and cross-regional integration is mostly missing. Border delays can be over 40 times higher in low-performing countries than in the best performing countries. Reducing travel times by one day would increase BRI trade by 5.2 percent.

- *International cooperation to improve connectivity makes economic sense.* Building a railway or a road has value for any country—but it also has spillover benefits to the countries around it. That may not to be taken into account if each country decides separately how to invest in infrastructure. Cross-border cooperation can further enhance the value of a country's investments—by adopting harmonized standards for infrastructure.

- *Estimated BRI debt financing is expected to be considerable for a handful of countries, including some with current debt vulnerabilities.* The cost of BRI transport projects in the 70 corridor economies (excluding China) is estimated to range between US$144 billion and US$304 billion. Estimated BRI investment including projects in all sectors, including energy, is worth US$575 billion. These investments take place in the context of rapidly rising public debts. External debt from outside the Paris Club, including debt from China, is low in many corridor economies, but it has increased in countries with a higher risk of debt distress.

**2. BRI transport projects can expand trade, increase foreign investment, and reduce poverty—by lowering trade costs. Yet, for some countries, the costs of new infrastructure could outweigh the gains.**

• *If fully implemented, BRI transport infrastructure can reduce travel times for economies along transport corridors by up to 12 percent, reducing trade costs.* In the rest of the world, travel times are estimated to fall by an average of 3 percent, showing that non-Belt and Road countries will also benefit from access to improved rails and ports in corridor economies. Precise estimation of the effects of the BRI is difficult, particularly due to the complexity of the initiative and the uncertainty surrounding many projects.

• *BRI transport projects are estimated to increase trade by between 2.8 and 9.7 percent for corridor economies and between 1.7 and 6.2 percent for the world.* Not all countries in the world would see positive trade effects, but aggregate effects are positive since all countries would experience a decline in trade costs due to the BRI's network effect. Sectors that are time-sensitive (such as fresh fruits and vegetables) or require time-sensitive inputs (such as electronics, chemicals and others integrated in global value chains) will be affected most, as countries specialize in new products. FDI inflows are expected to increase 7.6 percent for low-income corridor economies.

• *Increased trade is expected to increase global real income by 0.7 to 2.9 percent, not including the cost of infrastructure investment.* The largest gains are expected for corridor economies, with real income gains between 1.2 and 3.4 percent. Increases in FDI would further boost these effects.

• *BRI transport projects could contribute to lifting 7.6 million people from extreme poverty (less than $1.90 a day at purchasing power parity [PPP])* and 32 million people from moderate poverty (less than PPP$3.20 a day), mostly in corridor economies.

• *Reducing trade costs has the potential to reshape economic geography within and across countries, bringing gains from agglomeration.* For instance, a spatial analysis of Central and South Asia finds that real incomes in Pakistan could benefit from urban clustering and increasing returns in manufacturing. Cities in western China such as Urumqi are also likely to experience large gains in incomes, as are Kyrgyz Republic cities including Osh and Bishkek, which account for more than 40 percent of national income.

• *Income gains would be unevenly distributed across countries.* Real income gains in countries like the Kyrgyz Republic, Pakistan, and Thailand could be above 8 percent. But the analysis also finds that Azerbaijan, Mongolia, and Tajikistan could experience negative welfare effects because infrastructure costs would exceed gains from integration.

**3. Complementary policy reforms can maximize the positive effects of BRI transport projects and ensure that the gains are widely shared. For some countries, reforms are a precondition to having net gains from BRI transport projects.**

• *The value of individual transportation projects depends on the realization of others.* Project selection and appraisal and the inclusion of BRI projects in national development strategies is essential to avoid stranded infrastructure. Cooperation among participating countries can also ensure that projects are not redundant and that they maximize value from a regional perspective.

• *Real incomes for corridor economies could be an estimated two to four times larger if they implement reforms to reduce border delays and ease trade restrictions.* In landlocked Uzbekistan, average income gains from infrastructure improvements are estimated at less than 1 percent. But when complementary measures reduce border times, income gains rise to 9 percent.

• *Policy reforms facilitating trade, reducing trade policy barriers, and improving the management of corridors require country-specific actions and cooperation.* Supply-chain bottlenecks in a single country could block the potential benefit of the entire corridor in unlocking new trade opportunities. Deepening trade agreements among corridor economies could reduce the current fragmentation and establish the rules and mechanisms for trade and other policy reforms.

• *Increased private sector participation can help sustain the BRI in the long term. The initiative thus far has been driven predominantly by China's state-owned banks and state-owned enterprises.* To increase private sector participation in the BRI, participating countries will need to improve the investment climate and reduce the risks facing potential investors. Specific reforms include improving the regulatory environment and strengthening legal protection of investment through legal rules and their enforcement.

• *Complementary policies can help share the gains from BRI projects—including policies to strengthen social security, improve worker education and training, and increase labor mobility.* For the Belt and Road corridor economies as a whole, the BRI could displace about 12 million workers, mostly from the agricultural sector. Workers may also struggle to take advantage of opportunities that emerge in urban hubs or other places where economic activity concentrates. Such immobility or slow adjustment is likely to increase inequalities in real incomes.

**4. The BRI presents risks common to large infrastructure projects. These risks could be exacerbated by the limited transparency and openness of the initiative and the weak economic fundamentals and governance of several participating countries.**

• *Large infrastructure investments involving debt financing entail risks to debt sustainability.* An analysis that looks at all BRI debt (not just transport-related) shows that 12 of 43 low- and middle-income countries for which detailed data are available would experience a deterioration in their medium-term outlook for debt sustainability. This would occur even if BRI investments boosted growth. Assuming sound public investment management, favorable financing terms, and continued growth dividends, the BRI's impact on debt sustainability could be positive over the long term. There is thus a need to enhance the transparency of the terms and conditions of BRI projects and improve recipient countries' ability to assess these conditions. Comprehensive fiscal frameworks and improved regulatory environments can help ensure that projects are financed sustainably. China would also benefit from better coordination among different actors—government bodies, lending institutions, private sector firms, and state-owned enterprises—and having a debt restructuring framework in place that enables it to participate in a collaborative approach with other creditors.

• *Large infrastructure projects can create governance risks, including corruption and failures in public procurement.* The limited data available indicate that Chinese firms account for the majority of BRI contracts—according to one estimate, more than 60 percent of Chinese-funded BRI projects are allocated to Chinese companies. Little is known about the processes for selecting firms. Moving toward international good practices such as open and transparent public procurement would increase the likelihood that BRI projects are allocated to the firms best placed to implement them. Corruption risk varies across corridor economies and correlates closely with the quality of domestic institutions. Measures to reduce corruption include cooperation mechanisms to increase transparency in infrastructure projects and forms of community monitoring.

• *Large transport projects expose countries and local communities to environmental and social risks.* Many BRI routes pass through areas vulnerable to degradation, flooding, and landslides. Some portions pass through ecologically important but inadequately protected landscapes. Additional risks include increased pollution and illegal timber and wildlife trade risks. For instance, BRI transport infrastructure is estimated to increase carbon dioxide emissions by 0.3 percent worldwide—but by 7 percent or more in Cambodia, the Kyrgyz Republic, and the Lao People's Democratic Republic as production expands in sectors with higher emissions. Large infrastructure projects are also associated with an influx of workers, which may create risks of gender-based violence, sexually transmitted diseases, and social tensions. To address these concerns, it will be necessary—among other things—to conduct strategic environmental and social assessments of projects. Such assessments should be focused on the entire transportation corridor, taking advantage of the scale of the BRI to address cumulative direct and indirect risks.

**The Belt and Road Initiative, with its focus on connectivity and integration, has the potential to contribute to long-term development of the corridor economies analyzed in this study and beyond. Yet it also presents substantial challenges. Achieving its full potential will depend on the establishment of policies and institutions that will mitigate risks and support complementary reforms.**

The Belt and Road Initiative's main components—the Silk Road Economic Belt and the New Maritime Silk Road—evoke the ancient Silk Road, the quasi-mythical trade route spanning Asia, Europe, and East Africa as early as 200 BCE. The success of the ancient routes stemmed from two critical features (Frankopan 2017; Millward 2013). First, these "roads" were in fact a large transport network that not only linked East to West but also connected all points to the large landmass in the middle—Central, South, and West Asia. This contributed greatly to exchanges. Second, the ancient routes flourished when states ensured that transport infrastructure was efficient, communications across the network were open, the passage of goods and merchants was facilitated, and markets were organized. This supported trade not only in silk but also many other goods such as horses, paper, and cotton. History does not repeat itself, and the ancient Silk Road clearly was very different from the current trading system of complex modern economies. Yet these two features are worth recalling.

Collaboration between China and participating countries has led to efforts to improve customs-authority cooperation, investment protection, and corruption mitigation, among others. The 2nd Belt and Road Forum in April 2019 was an important milestone, with the launch of several new collaborative efforts. But more needs to be done in multilateral cooperation and domestic policy reform—including better coordination and practices within China. Urgent action is required to improve the transparency and data for BRI projects, the openness and functioning of markets, and the monitoring and enforcement of standards. A full list of recommended reforms and their sequencing is provided on table 5.1.

**Bolder and deeper policy reforms will be required for the current realities to catch up with the ambitions of the Belt and Road Initiative. Reforms and actions should be based on three core principles for corridor economies, including China:**

• The first is transparency. Providing more public information on project planning, fiscal costs and budgeting, and procurement will improve the effectiveness of individual infrastructure investments and national development strategies. Greater transparency is essential to encourage community involvement and build public trust in investment decisions.

• The second is country-specific reform. Many countries have trade policies and border management practices that inhibit cross-border trade. Making it easier to import and export goods is essential for countries to reap the full benefits of BRI investments. All corridor economies would benefit from open procurement processes, stronger governance, and fiscal and debt sustainability frameworks that allow them to fully account for the potential costs of debt-financed infrastructure. Given the risks associated with BRI corridors, countries can also invest in complementary adjustment policies, social and environmental safety nets, investments in other skills and infrastructure, and mobile labor.

• The third is multilateral cooperation, including coordination across BRI projects. For countries to fully benefit from the positive spillovers of economic corridor development, they will need to work together—including through existing regional and multilateral organizations—to improve trade facilitation and border management, unify standards in building infrastructure, agree on legal standards and investor protections that will encourage further investment along BRI corridors, and manage environmental risks.

# CHAPTER 1

Connectivity, trade,
and debt in the Belt
and Road corridor economies

Belt and Road corridor economies account for a large share of global economic output, trade, and investment. Merchandise trade across corridor economies alone accounts for 40 percent of global trade. In trade, foreign direct investment, and participation in global value chains, corridor economies have made big strides in attracting investment and integrating globally.

But these gains are unevenly distributed across regions and countries. Many countries— particularly the small, landlocked, and fragile—remain largely outside the global trading system. They trade and attract investment at rates well below their potential. Underlying the challenges are poor infrastructure and inefficient policies. The density and quality of transport infrastructure and services are highly uneven, resulting in above-average trade costs and trading times. And policies that would boost trade and investment remain more restrictive, and trade agreements less comprehensive, than for high-income countries. International cooperation can help countries to close these gaps, but new infrastructure is built in a context of rapidly rising public debt.

## 1.1 CURRENT TRADE AND FOREIGN DIRECT INVESTMENT LANDSCAPE

On average, Belt and Road corridor economies are active in international trade, including through engagement in global value chains (GVCs.) They are also important destinations for foreign direct investment (FDI). But the aggregate picture can be misleading, and the divergences among corridor economies are wide. They include top performers, some having seen their shares in global exports and FDI rise through increased integration in global value chains. But many remain at the margin of global markets. Indeed, corridor economies undertrade by 30 percent and fall short of absorbing potential FDI by 70 percent.

### Trade in goods

Belt and Road corridor economies accounted for almost 40 percent of the global merchandise exports in 2017, close to five times higher than in 2000. But this impressive growth in trade masks disparities (figure 1.1). Exports of economies in East Asia and Pacific and Europe and Central Asia now account for more than 80 percent of Belt and Road corridor economies' exports of goods.[1] Although economies in South Asia and the Middle East and North Africa and the two Sub-Saharan corridor economies have seen their shares in global exports pick up since the mid-2000s, their export values are much lower than those of Europe and Central Asia and especially East Asia and Pacific.[2]

---

[1] As Boffa (2018) shows, these regions are even better performers when it comes to exports of intermediate goods, indicating a link between their dynamism and their engagement in GVCs.

[2] Similar analyses of corridor economies' goods imports reveal the same patterns.

**Figure 1.1:** Trade of Belt and Road corridor economies, by region, 1990-2016

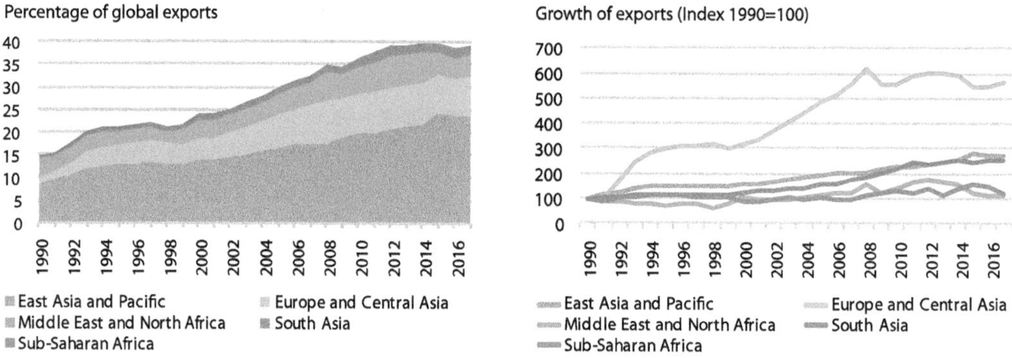

Percentage of global exports

Growth of exports (Index 1990=100)

- East Asia and Pacific
- Middle East and North Africa
- Sub-Saharan Africa
- Europe and Central Asia
- South Asia

- East Asia and Pacific
- Middle East and North Africa
- Sub-Saharan Africa
- Europe and Central Asia
- South Asia

*Source:* IMF, Direction of Trade Statistics.

Within each region, corridor economies vary widely in the scale and growth of exports.

- Corridor economies in East Asia and Pacific include China, the world's largest merchandise exporter since 2009, but also Timor-Leste, with the smallest export value of all corridor economies.[3] On dynamism, corridor economies in the region include Vietnam and Cambodia, with exports growing more than 10 percent a year since 2000, but also the Philippines and Brunei Darussalam, with exports growing at less than 4 percent a year between 2000 and 2017.

- Europe and Central Asia also has large BRI exporters, such as the Russian Federation and Turkey, and small exporters, such as Armenia, the Kyrgyz Republic, Moldova, and Tajikistan, with less than US$3 billion of merchandise exports in 2017. There are dynamic exporters, such as Bosnia and Herzegovina and Lithuania, and lagging ones, notably, Tajikistan, with 2017 exports just a little ahead of 2000's.

- In the Middle East and North Africa in 2017, half the exports of corridor economies were accounted for by Saudi Arabia and the United Arab Emirates, with more than US$200 billion each. The smallest exporters included Djibouti, the Syrian Arab Republic, and the Republic of Yemen. The last two conflict-stricken countries had negative export growth from 2000 to 2017. In contrast, exports grew the fastest in Bahrain, Lebanon, and Qatar.

- In South Asia, India is by far the largest exporter. Its export values in 2017 were nine times larger than those of Bangladesh, the runner-up in the group. At the opposite extreme, countries with the smallest exports include Bhutan and Maldives. Bhutan grew the fastest from 2000 to 2017, followed by India and Bangladesh. Relative laggards in export growth included Nepal, growing at 0.4 percent, and Sri Lanka, at 4 percent.

---

[3] In 2017, China's merchandise exports of US$2.3 trillion accounted for 55 percent of corridor economies' exports. That amount was four times larger than the export value of Hong Kong SAR, China, and six times larger than that of the Russian Federation, the second- and third-largest exporters among Belt and Road corridor economies.

**Figure 1.2:** Trade integration of Belt and Road corridor economies and the role of China

**a.** Share of BRI destinations in Belt and Road corridor economies' goods exports, by region

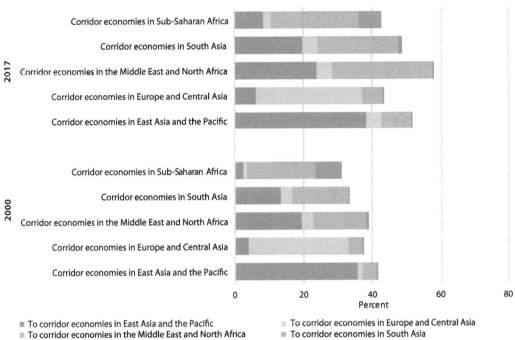

• In Sub-Saharan Africa, Kenya exported US$6 billion in 2017 and had annual growth of 7 percent from 2000 to 2017. Tanzania exported US$4 billion, with 10 percent annual growth. With trade representing less than 30 percent of GDP, Kenya and Tanzania were among the least open corridor economies in 2017.

Over time, corridor economies have been trading more with each other. Yet integration within the BRI group is not diffused evenly. Two major pockets of deeper integration can be distinguished, one for corridor economies in East Asia and Pacific and the other for those in Europe and Central Asia (figure 1.2a). Indeed, most of the exports and imports of these two groups are intraregional (more than 30 percent for exports in 2017) and have been so for decades. At the other extreme, corridor economies in South Asia seem to be the least integrated intraregionally. On flows between regions, corridor economies in Europe and Central Asia are the least integrated. Corridor economies in East Asia and Pacific appear to be the most integrated, due in great part to China, which has become more central to the trade links among corridor economies in recent years (figure 1.2b).[4]

_____

[4] The patterns of imports are generally similar, except for the two countries in Sub-Saharan Africa, for which the Middle East and North Africa was more important as an origin of imports than the other regions in 2000, and East Asia and Pacific was more important in 2017.

**b.** Share of China in goods exports and imports of Belt and Road corridor economies, by region

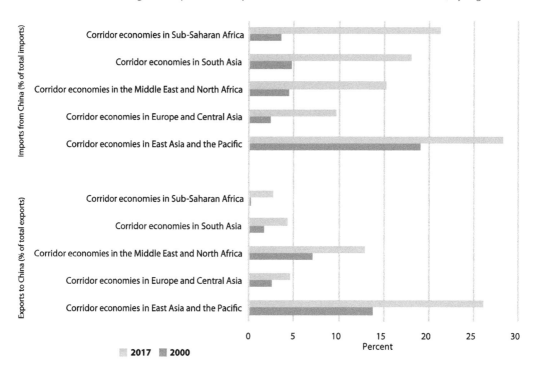

*Source:* IMF, Direction of Trade Statistics.
*Note:* For each region, the rest (up to 100 percent) is accounted for by non–Belt and Road corridor economies. Corridor economies in Sub-Saharan Africa include only Kenya and Tanzania.

## Foreign direct investment

The share of global FDI flows that went to Belt and Road corridor economies as a destination has fluctuated around 35 percent since the global financial crisis, with the group absorbing almost US$600 billion in 2017 (Chen and Lin 2018). Furthermore, corridor economies' direct investment abroad amounted to almost US$400 million in 2017, or 25 percent of global FDI, up from less than 10 percent in 2000.

Similar to trade, FDI flows by region provide a different picture (figure 1.3). East Asia and Pacific is the main FDI recipient as well as the driver of FDI outflows. Europe and Central Asia is second, trailing East Asia and Pacific by a large and growing gap. In general, corridor economies with higher income attract more investment and are more likely to invest abroad. Indeed, high- and upper-middle-income groups have accounted for 80 percent of FDI inflows and over 90 percent of outflows in recent years. Most other corridor economies, particularly low-income economies, fare poorly in attracting FDI.

**Figure 1.3:** Belt and Road corridor economies' direct investment, by region

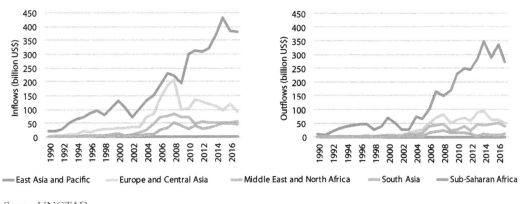

*Source:* UNCTAD.

Within regions, as well, FDI flows show significant heterogeneity and concentration. Only a handful of corridor economies absorbed more than US$10 billion in FDI in 2017. They include China; Hong Kong SAR, China; Indonesia; Singapore; and Vietnam in East Asia and Pacific; the Russian Federation and Turkey in Europe and Central Asia; and Israel and the United Arab Emirates in the Middle East and North Africa. Together, these economies accounted for almost 80 percent of the total FDI to corridor economies in 2017. In contrast, for many corridor economies, FDI is less than 1 percent of GDP. This group includes Bangladesh, Bhutan, Brunei Darussalam, Kenya, Nepal, Pakistan, Timor-Leste, and Uzbekistan.

The concentration of direct investment outflows is even starker: just eight economies accounted for 87 percent of the total flows out of corridor economies in 2017. Five of these eight are from East Asia and Pacific: China; Hong Kong SAR, China; Singapore; Taiwan, China; and Thailand. The others are India, the Russian Federation, and the United Arab Emirates. At the other extreme, five of 13 corridor economies in East Asia and Pacific and the majority in the other regions invested less than US$1 billion abroad in 2017.

The majority of corridor economies' FDI inflows come from non-corridor economies (figure 1.4). Yet, as for trade, the share of corridor economies is growing, in great part due to investment from China, which has picked up since the mid-2000s. Furthermore, China started to gain share in 2008, on the back of the significant drop in investment from developed countries during the global financial crisis. Chinese firms seized the opportunities to invest while firms from developed countries pulled back (Chen and Lin 2018).

**Figure 1.4:** Foreign direct investment in Belt and Road corridor economies, by source

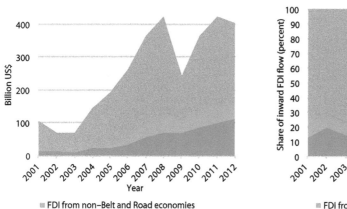
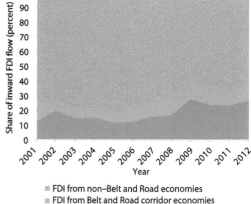

■ FDI from non–Belt and Road economies
■ FDI from Belt and Road corridor economies
■ FDI from China

■ FDI from non–Belt and Road economies
■ FDI from Belt and Road corridor economies
■ FDI from China

*Source:* Chen and Lin 2018.

## Participation in global value chains

Belt and Road corridor economies have increased their GVC participation and are moving up the value chain (figure 1.5).[5] Backward participation of corridor economies, as proxied by the total foreign value added embodied in their exports, amounted to about 24 percent of gross exports in 2015, down 4 percentage points from the average for corridor economies during the precrisis 2000s. Forward participation, measured as the domestic value added embodied in other economies' gross exports, stayed at around 28 percent since 2011, having increased steadily from about 22 percent in the early 1990s.

Corridor economies in East Asia and Pacific and Europe and Central Asia are highly integrated via backward participation and drive the BRI average due to a large trading scale. But a closer look at country data shows that for both regions, GVC backward participation is driven by few economies, such as China, Malaysia, and Singapore in East Asia, and the Czech Republic, Estonia, and Hungary in Europe and Central Asia. GVC participation of corridor economies in other regions is substantially lower. The Middle East and North Africa and Europe and Central Asia have higher forward participation, but this mostly reflects important commodity exporters such as Kazakhstan, the Russian Federation, and Saudi Arabia.

---

[5] Given data limitations, the importance of GVCs for all corridor economies is hard to gauge with accuracy (Boffa 2018).

**Figure 1.5:** Belt and Road corridor economies' participation in GVCs, by region

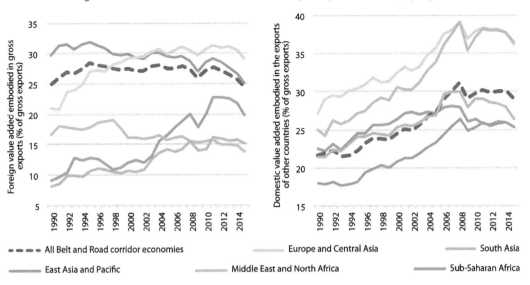

*Source:* Eora Multiregional Input-Output Table.
*Note:* Gross exports and backward and forward participation encompass both goods and services.

Backward and forward linkages of corridor economies are still dominated by non–Belt and Road countries, but the share of corridor economies has been gradually increasing over time. For backward participation, corridor economies accounted for 33 percent of the total foreign value added embodied in corridor economies' gross exports in 2011, up from 24 percent in 1995. For forward participation, the domestic value added originating in corridor economies embodied in the exports of other corridor economies represented 43 percent of the domestic value added embodied in the exports of both other Belt and Road and non–Belt and Road economies in 2011, up from 36 percent in 1995.

Over time, China has established itself as a more central player in the GVC network linking corridor economies. All regions experienced a gradual rise in the share of Chinese value added in their own imports, and a rise in the share of China in their domestic value added embodied in other economies' exports (Boffa 2018). Moreover, judged by the number of countries ranking China among the three most important sources of foreign value added used to produce exports, it had grown into a significant gravitational center for corridor economies already by 2010 (figure 1.6). Consistent with this finding, trade and investment relations of China with corridor economies started intensifying well before the formal announcement of the BRI in 2013 (box 1.1).

**Figure 1.6:** The centrality of China as a source of foreign value added in Belt and Road corridor economies' gross exports

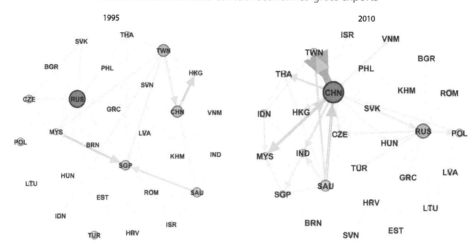

*Source:* Boffa 2018, based on Organisation for Economic Cooperation and Development, Trade in Value Added database.
*Note:* Exports refer here to both goods and services. The size of an economy's node is the total number of times for which it was among the top three sources of value added for each of its partners. The thickness of the edges represents the strength of the link in value added.

---

**Box 1.1:** How old is the BRI?

The Belt and Road Initiative (BRI) was officially announced in 2013 during President Xi Jinping's visits to Kazakhstan in September and Indonesia in October. Trade data show that China's exports, particularly of infrastructure-related goods, had started flowing to Belt and Road corridor economies for a decade before the official launch of the initiative. Moreover, by 2013, China was already actively engaged in construction contracts in corridor economies. The 2013 announcement of the BRI was not a dramatic shift, but it brought new energy to ongoing trends in China's trade relations.

First, trade data indicate that the group of corridor economies as a whole had already seen more than a decade-long steady rise in importance as a destination for Chinese exports (figure B1.1.1). They accounted collectively for about 40 percent of China's overall merchandise exports in 2017, up almost 9 percentage points since 2001. Gains in the share of corridor economies in China's exports of infrastructure-related goods amounted to 11 percentage points, and gains in corridor economies' share of iron and steel exported from China were 16 percentage points. The gains were driven mostly by corridor economies where BRI transport infrastructure projects are being built or planned (called the BRI "core" in figure B1.1.1). In 2017, these countries accounted for 27 and 37 percent of China's exports of infrastructure-related goods and of iron and steel respectively, and had already gained 15 and 17 percentage points in these respective shares by 2013. Moreover, at least for some of these economies (not only those in developing East Asia), trade data show an increased dynamism of China's exports of infrastructure-related goods around 2013 (Constantinescu and Ruta 2018).

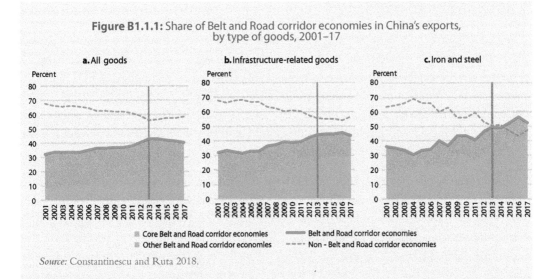

**Figure B1.1.1:** Share of Belt and Road corridor economies in China's exports, by type of goods, 2001–17

*Source:* Constantinescu and Ruta 2018.

Second, corridor economies accounted for a larger share of Chinese construction investment than non–Belt and Road countries even before 2013 (Chen and Lin 2018). China's overall outward investment in corridor economies increased substantially after 2013, but the volume of China's outward investment in non–Belt and Road countries increased more rapidly than the volume of investment in corridor economies. Yet for China's construction contracts abroad, the picture is different. They show a similar upward trend, but corridor economies account for a much larger share in China's construction contracts overseas than in China's foreign direct investment. Since 2009, the share of corridor economies has systematically exceeded the share of non–Belt and Road countries in China's construction projects (figure B1.1.2).

**Figure B1.1.2:** Trends in China's outward investment and construction contracts

**a. China's outward investment**

**b. China's outward construction**

— Belt and Road corridor economies      — Non-Belt and Road corridor economies

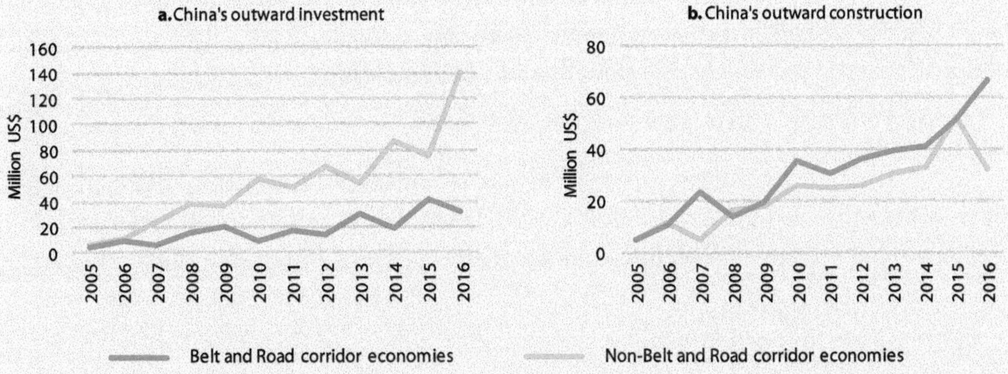

*Source:* Chen and Lin 2018.

### *Missing trade and FDI*

Belt and Road corridor economies have trade and FDI relations below their potential. Corridor economies undertrade with each other and with the rest of the world by 30 percent on average (Baniya, Rocha, and Ruta 2018).[6] And as recipients of FDI, corridor economies fall short of their absorptive potential by 70 percent (Chen and Lin 2018). These findings suggest that barriers to trade and FDI in the form of infrastructure or policy gaps reduce the potential trade and FDI flows that could be realized by corridor economies. These gaps are analyzed in the rest of this chapter.

The estimates of missing trade and FDI for corridor economies are considerable. An important question is how much improvements in transportation infrastructure and other policy reforms that reduce trade times could boost trade and FDI for corridor economies. A one-day decrease in trading times would increase exports among corridor economies by 5.2 percent on average (Baniya, Rocha, and Ruta 2018). And a 10 percent decrease in trading time is associated with a 12 percent increase in FDI flows to corridor economies (Chen and Lin 2018). These findings suggest that infrastructure improvements and policy reforms that can alleviate impediments to trade and FDI could have a big impact on integrating corridor economies with world markets.

## 1.2 INFRASTRUCTURE AND POLICY GAPS

Physical and policy barriers may constrain the connectivity of many Belt and Road corridor economies.

### *Transport and digital connectivity*

Transport and digital connections complement each other in allowing people from different locations to exchange goods, ideas, and knowledge through physical and virtual interactions. Without efficient transport connections, the potential of e-commerce would be greatly diminished. Just-in-time supply chains rely as much on the timely transmission of information as on the timely transportation of inputs and outputs.

#### Transport infrastructure and services

The quality of road and rail infrastructure presents contrasting patterns across Belt and Road corridor economies. Countries to the north and northwest of China are perceived to have very low-quality roads, while China, and the countries to

---

[6] The estimates for missing trade and FDI were obtained by comparing actual trade and FDI values with potential ones, given the predictions of the gravity model, a tool strongly endorsed for analyzing trade and FDI due to its predictive power (Head and Mayer 2014).

**Figure 1.7:** Quality of land infrastructure

**a.** Quality of road infrastructure                    **b.** Quality of rail infrastructure

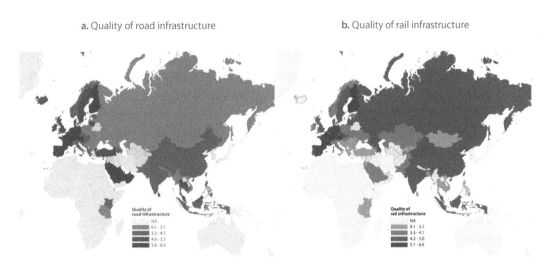

*Source:* World Economic Forum 2018.
*Note:* Western European countries are included as comparators because most BRI infrastructure projects are on the Eurasia transport network, and a network is only as good as its weakest link.

its southwest form a "corridor" of relatively good road quality (figure 1.7a). Some Southeast Asian countries are also perceived as having relatively good road quality. But only Malaysia and some Gulf countries are perceived as having high-quality roads, as in Western European countries. The quality of rail infrastructure mirrors the quality of road infrastructure (figure 1.7b). The Russian Federation, Kazakhstan, Ukraine, the Slovak Republic, and the Czech Republic form a corridor of relatively good rail infrastructure, while most Southeast Asian countries and the countries southwest of China, such as the Kyrgyz Republic and Pakistan, are perceived as having some of the lower quality rail infrastructure. Across corridor economies, logistics professionals perceive gaps in rail infrastructure as more prevalent than gaps in road infrastructure. Seaport and airport infrastructure receive higher marks for perceived quality (Wiederer 2018).

Year-round access to transport is limited outside urban areas in corridor economies. In most countries, the road network provides the broadest coverage of all transport infrastructure. But having access to a road does not guarantee that people will be able to travel and exchange goods, ideas, and knowledge all year. For people to benefit from regional and global integration requires access to at least an all-weather road. Most urban roads provide year-round access. The Rural Accessibility Index, which captures the proportion of rural population living within 2 kilometers of an all-weather road, is the standard metric for year-round access. While in most developed economies close to 100 percent of the rural population lives within 2 kilometers of an all-weather road, in most corridor economies less than 65 percent do, and in Central Asian countries less than 32 percent (Rozenberg and Fay 2019).[7]

The availability of maritime shipping services in coastal corridor economies between China and Western Europe varies. From a global trade perspective, the availability of maritime shipping services is important. China; Hong Kong SAR, China; Malaysia; and Singapore are among the five economies enjoying the highest supply of maritime shipping services as measured by the Liner Shipping Connectivity Index (figure 1.8a).[8] These economies are followed by Germany, the Netherlands, the United Kingdom, and the United States. Oman, Poland, Sri Lanka, and Turkey are corridor economies with above-average access to shipping services, while Bulgaria, Cambodia, Estonia, Georgia, and Myanmar are among those with the lowest access.

There are large differences in logistics performance across the corridor economies as measured by the World Bank's 2018 Logistics Performance Index (LPI). Quality infrastructure and availability of services are prerequisites for good connectivity, but they are not enough. High-quality services are also needed for timely and cost-effective transportation. Three of the bottom 20 LPI performers are corridor economies (Afghanistan, Bhutan, and Iraq), as are three of the top 20 performers (Hong Kong SAR, China; Singapore; and the United Arab Emirates). The competence and quality of rail service providers is rated as lower than the competence and quality of service provided by road, maritime, and air transport providers. Warehousing, transloading, and distribution services are rated comparatively high as well (Wiederer 2018). A challenge for China is that it is surrounded by several economies with low perceived logistics performance (figure 1.8b).

The seamless regional integration of national transport infrastructure and transport services is crucial, and gaps can explain why trade and investment flows between corridor economies are below potential. The railway networks in South and Southeast Asia were developed by colonial governments with the goal of transporting cargo to and from the seaports, not to connect countries. In some countries, the rail network continued to expand, but with a domestic focus. In other countries, such as Bangladesh and Myanmar, the rail network has not received adequate maintenance or upgrade investments. In the economies forming the Commonwealth of Independent States (CIS), the rail network was developed during the late 19th and early 20th century, first under the Tsar and then the Soviet Union, with the goal

---

[7] An all-weather road is motorable all year by the prevailing means of rural transport. The Liner Shipping Connectivity Index is computed by the United Nations Conference on Trade and Development based on five components of the maritime transport sector: number of ships, their container-carrying capacity, maximum vessel size, number of services, and number of companies that deploy container ships in a country's ports.

[8] The Liner Shipping Connectivity Index is computed by the United Nations Conference on Trade and Development based on five components of the maritime transport sector: number of ships, their container-carrying capacity, maximum vessel size, number of services, and number of companies that deploy container ships in a country's ports.

**Figure 1.8:** Transport and logistics services in Belt and Road corridor economies

**a.** Liner Shipping Connectivity Index          **b.** Logistics Performance Index

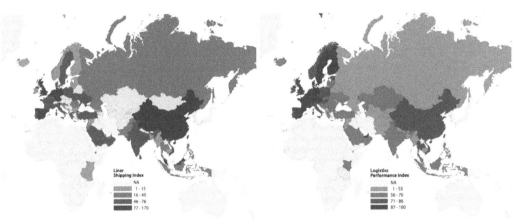

*Source:* UNCTAD and Logistics Performance Index 2018.
*Note:* Western European countries are included as comparators because most BRI infrastructure projects are on the Eurasia transport network, and a network is only as good as its weakest link.

of connecting economic centers to Moscow and to each other (Djankov and Freund 2002). Although it has different gauges, fragmented electrification, and varied quality due to uneven maintenance, it is still the best integrated rail network among the corridor economies.

Bottlenecks differ along the three rail routes connecting China to Central Asia and Europe. The northern and central routes go through Russia, and the southern route goes through Kazakhstan across the Caspian Sea to Turkey or Georgia. Most of the northern routes have been improved over the past 15–20 years. The main constraint between China and Eastern Europe along the northern route is in Mongolia, where the lines are single-tracked and in poor condition. All three routes are constrained by railway track gauge changes, differences in allowable axle loading, and partial electrification (Bullock, Liu, and Tan 2018). Another bottleneck in the northern and southern routes is the insufficient capacity of European railways, including transshipment facilities, especially in Poland. All southern routes face difficulties in eastern Turkey because of the rugged terrain around Kars and in the west because of the need for ferry crossings, so no regular rail service uses the southern routes all the way to Europe (Bullock, Liu, and Tan 2018).

Block train container services between China and Europe (along the northern and central routes), between China and Afghanistan, and recently between China and Vietnam have offset some of the constraints and reduced transport costs (Bullock, Liu, and Tan 2018). Sending freight across borders in individual wagonloads (freight cars) has been possible for quite some time but was prone to long delays waiting for connections, and especially for other processes such as transshipment or customs inspections of individual wagons. Block container services are much cheaper to operate than wagonload services since all wagons in a train carry the same commodity and are shipped from the same origin to the same destination. The result: a steady reduction in travel time over the past five years and a major increase in competitiveness.

With the capital requirements for road development lower than for rail, corridor economies have more regional roads than rail connections. Mongolian roads connecting China and Russia are not in good condition, mainly due to poor maintenance and harsh weather. In Central Asia and Eastern Europe, inadequate maintenance is a greater problem than missing links or insufficient capacity (Rastogi and Arvis 2014; Linn and Zucker 2019). Under the ASEAN and Greater Mekong Subregion initiatives, road connectivity within Southeast Asia has substantially improved, including cross-border links. Some missing and weak road links remain in and between Myanmar and Lao PDR. In South Asia, the world's least integrated region, the conditions and capacities of roads reaching borders and border crossings have received very limited attention since independence. This is slowly changing, but South Asia has some of the weakest links.

Even though China is closer to Southeast Asia and South Asia than to Europe, the physical connectivity with the Asian regions is weaker. Due to poor-quality land infrastructure and level of service, almost all freight between China and Southeast and South Asia goes by sea. The transport infrastructure in Myanmar is so poor that virtually no traffic flows overland to it. China's only land connectivity with South Asia is through the Himalayas. China connects with Pakistan by road over the Khunjerab Pass at an altitude of 4,600 meters, but the road is open only for seven months of the year. China–Nepal–India connectivity is very limited due to the poor infrastructure in Nepal and the need for four transshipments along the route.

## Digital infrastructure and services

Many people in Belt and Road corridor economies remain untouched by the digital revolution. The share of population using the internet is below 55 percent in most Asian countries, though Malaysia, Singapore, Kazakhstan, and countries in the Arabian Peninsula are among the exceptions (figure 1.9). Even in China, which has the largest number of internet users, over 45 percent of the population do not use it. Moreover, "the digital divide within countries can be as high as that between countries" (World Bank 2016c).

There are two poles to fourth-generation (4G) mobile signal coverage among corridor economies, according to the latest data available from the Sustainable Development Goals indicators (see figure 1.9). Worldwide, 56 percent of internet traffic is through mobile devices (We Are Social 2018), so deployment and coverage of mobile broadband

**Figure 1.9:** Internet users and access to mobile broadband

**a.** Internet users (percentage of population)                    **b.** 4G coverage (percentage of population)

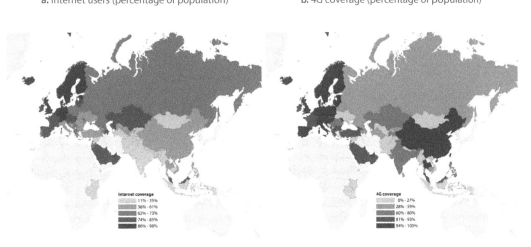

*Source:* World Development Indicators and https://unstats.un.org/sdgs/indicators/database/.
*Note:* Western European countries are included as comparators because most BRI infrastructure projects are on the Eurasia network, and a network is only as good as its weakest link.

networks provide a good picture of internet infrastructure and access. Among corridor economies, China, Thailand, and Eastern European countries have the largest share of population with access to a 4G mobile signal. Countries in the Arabian Peninsula also have high 4G coverage. But the rest of the countries in Asia, particularly landlocked ones, have low 4G coverage—that could partly explain the low share of internet users in those countries.

Countries bordering China would benefit from better connectivity through global submarine cables. Existing international internet bandwidth is quite low, particularly for landlocked countries, where BRI connectivity could provide an outlet to global submarine cables (Kelly 2018). Cross-border fiber optic connectivity with China would also provide redundancy for landlocked countries, as only a small portion of their international bandwidth comes from connectivity with China. For example, 8 percent of the Kyrgyz Republic's total international bandwidth and 4 percent of Tajikistan's come through overland connections with China. In South Asia, Afghanistan and Bhutan have no connections with China, and 4 percent of Nepal's international internet capacity is through the fiber optic connection to China, launched in January 2018.

**Table 1.1:** Average pre-BRI trading times within and between regions

| Average shipping time (days) | Central and Eastern Europe | Central and Western Africa | East Asia and Pacific | Middle East and North Africa | South Asia | Sub-Saharan Africa |
|---|---|---|---|---|---|---|
| Central and Eastern Europe | 3.3 | | | | | |
| Central and Western Asia | 13.4 | 13.0 | | | | |
| East Asia and Pacific | 26.8 | 22.5 | 7.1 | | | |
| Middle East and North Africa | 12.8 | 15.4 | 20.4 | 9.0 | | |
| South Asia | 22.4 | 20.3 | 15.5 | 15.2 | 11.8 | |
| Sub-Saharan Africa | 19.8 | 23.2 | 20.6 | 14.4 | 17.6 | 4.0 |
| **Regional** | **13.9** | **16.6** | **19.6** | **14.0** | **17.8** | **18.5** |

*Source:* de Soyres et al. 2018.
*Note:* Averaged over all country-pairs in each region-pair.

## Network connectivity among Belt and Road corridor economies

The limited availability of quality transport infrastructure and services across some Belt and Road corridor economies translates into long travel times. De Soyres et al. (2018) have estimated the shipping times—including border crossing times—between BRI locations using geographic information system (GIS) analysis. The East Asia and Pacific region has longer shipping times than the other regions (table 1.1), particularly with Central and Eastern Europe, and Central and Western Asia. For example, it takes on average more than 30 days to ship goods between China and countries in Central and Eastern Europe, such as Croatia, Estonia, and Poland. Shipping times between China and Central Asian countries such as Georgia and Armenia are also long at 32 days, on average. (See chapter 2 for the changes in shipping times as a result of BRI transport interventions.)

The limited availability of quality transport infrastructure and services across some corridor economies also translates into higher transport costs. The cost to ship a container to Rotterdam and Shanghai (proxies for Western Europe and China) varies across Europe and Central Asia (figure 1.10). Central Asian countries face the highest costs,[9] while Turkey and Greece face some of the lowest costs. The average cost for shipping a

---

[9] While Central Asian countries are poorly connected to Shanghai, they may be better connected to western and central China.

**Figure 1.10:** Cost to ship a container to Rotterdam and Shanghai from Belt and Road corridor economies

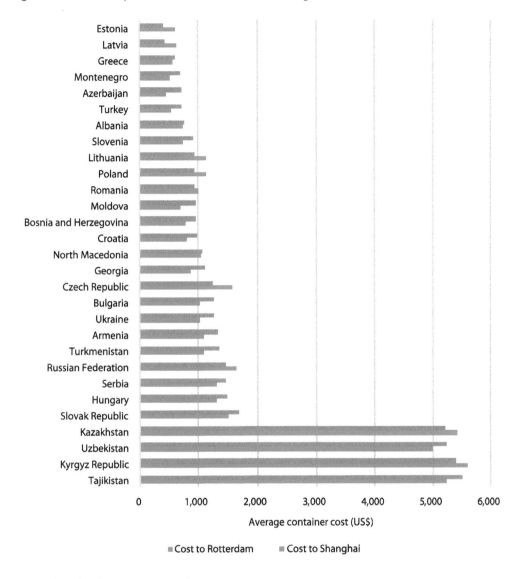

*Source:* Lebrand and Briceño-Garmendia 2018.

container to neighboring countries is the highest in Russia, Turkey, and Central Asian countries, and lowest in Western Balkan countries (figure 1.11).[10]

---

[10] Lebrand and Briceño-Garmendia (2018) use the average of all countries sharing a border.

**Figure 1.11:** Average regional cost to ship a container to neighboring economies

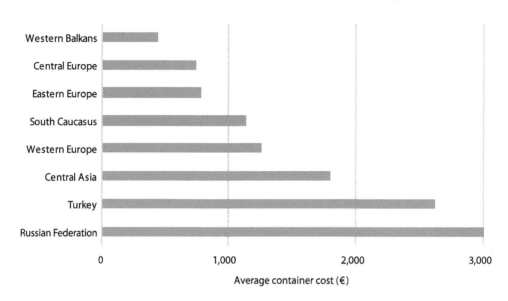

*Source:* Lebrand and Briceño-Garmendia 2018.

Network analysis techniques can assess the effectiveness of the transport network connecting China, Central Asian, and European countries (Lebrand and Briceño-Garmendia 2018). The Eurasian transport network provides people and firms in China with better access to foreign markets than to people and firms in Central Asian and European countries. Countries in the Caucasus and Central Asia are the least connected to economic activity in other countries. The last finding is partly explained by the landlockedness of some countries in the Caucasus and Central Asia and the limited shipping connectivity of the coastal countries. China is the most critical node in the Eurasia transport network, thanks to its maritime connectivity and the low cost of maritime shipping. Russia is the third most critical country after Germany in the Eurasia transport network and the most critical in the network connecting Central Asia with Europe. Many BRI projects will provide Central Asian countries alternative trade routes.

A look at the connectivity between cities or economic centers in Asia shows a strong imprint of national borders. On the effectiveness of the transport and digital networks in allowing people and information to travel between Asian cities, Chinese cities are better connected with each other than with other cities in Asia (Derudder, Lia, and Kunaka 2018). Indian and Indonesian cities show a similar pattern. Only cities in Association of Southeast Asian Nations (ASEAN) countries are strongly connected to cities in other ASEAN countries.

## Transport and digital infrastructure needs

The connectivity infrastructure needs are substantial in Belt and Road corridor economies. Average transport investment needs to satisfy future mobility demand in Asia and the former Soviet Union amount to 0.5–1 percent of GDP per year until 2030 (Rozenberg and Fay 2019).[11] The Asian Development Bank projects that average infrastructure investment needs in developing Asia will be about 5.9 percent of GDP per year until 2030 (ADB 2017).[12] Investments in transport represent 32 percent of the needs, and investments in telecommunications, 9 percent.[13] The International Transport Forum (2016) forecasts that by 2030 container traffic across corridor economies will increase most in South Asia (193 percent) and in Southeast Asia (163 percent), with container traffic in 2030 in South Asia 93 percent higher than container port capacity in 2013, and in Southeast Asia, 86 percent higher.

The solution is not necessarily to spend more, but to spend better on the right objectives (Rozenberg and Fay 2019). Spending better means focusing on the service gap rather than the infrastructure gap—and improving service typically requires much more than just capital expenditure. It also means carefully examining operation and maintenance implications when considering capital investments. The earlier discussion highlighted the need to spend on the operations and maintenance of existing assets and develop services that reduce connectivity costs (as with block train container services). On one estimate, the maintenance needs in Asia and the former Soviet Union amount to about 2 percent of GDP per year until 2030, or more than twice the capital investment needs (Rozenberg and Fay 2019).

The infrastructure gaps in corridor economies leads to the question of selecting the right projects to fill these gaps. The transport investment needs depend on each economy's context, economic growth aspirations, and social and environmental objectives. The right set of interventions should be based on robust analysis of their costs, benefits, and risks. To help policymakers set the right objectives and select the best interventions, chapters 2–4 discus potential economic, environmental, and social impacts and risks of currently proposed BRI transport infrastructure.

---

[11] The projections are based on a global model that captures the intertwined evolution of technical systems, energy demand behavior, and economic growth in a computable general equilibrium framework with bottom-up sectoral modules. The model incorporates assumptions about growth drivers, consumer preferences, spatial organization, climate change mitigation policies, and technical challenges to mitigation policies.

[12] These estimates do not include cross-border infrastructure.

[13] The ADB (2017) projections are based on an econometric model that estimates the relationship between physical infrastructure stocks and key economic and demographic factors in developing Asia from 1970 to 2011, which then are adjusted to include climate change mitigation and adaptation measures. They are based on assumptions about shifts in economic activity, structure, and demographics.

## *Policies and institutions*

Policy gaps, in addition to the infrastructure gaps, explain the poor integration of several Belt and Road corridor economies with regional and global markets. Four sets of policies and institutions that can affect the integration of corridor economies are related to trade facilitation, tariffs and nontariff barriers, restrictions on FDI, and trade agreements.

### Trade facilitation

Inefficient trade procedures are a major source of trade costs, and trade facilitation reform is intended to streamline trade procedures while ensuring that border agencies can achieve revenue, safety, and community protection objectives. On average, Belt and Road corridor economies fare considerably worse than Group of Seven (G7) countries in border delays, which are key targets of trade facilitation. The time to import reported by the World Bank's Doing Business ranges from twice that in the G7 for the average corridor economy in Europe and Central Asia—to 44 times that in the G7 for the average corridor economy in Sub-Saharan Africa (figure 1.12). The time to export for corridor economies is also higher than in the G7, but the gaps are much smaller. For example, Sub-Saharan time to export is only five times that in the G7 and three times that in Europe and Central Asia.[14]

An analysis of the six overland BRI corridors using a wide range of trade facilitation indicators shows that they tend to perform below global averages (Bartley Johns et al. 2018).

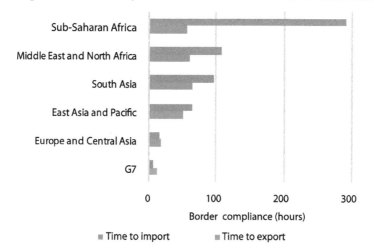

**Figure 1.12:** Time to import for Belt and Road corridor economies and the G7

*Source:* World Bank Doing Business Survey 2019.
*Note:* G7 = Group of Seven.

---

[14] The Doing Business reports the time to export/import through the main gateway in a country. Because BRI corridors in most cases do not go through these main gateways, actual export and import times may be longer than those reported here.

• Times to comply with regulatory and border requirements for imports are higher than global averages on all corridors except the New Eurasian Corridor, and times to export are higher than the global average on all corridors except the New Eurasian and China–Pakistan corridors (figure 1.13). The gap between import and export times is higher than the global average on all but two corridors (the China–Mongolia–Russia Corridor and China–Indochina Peninsula Economic Corridor), suggesting a disproportionate burden for traders importing in corridor economies.

• Customs and border management agency performance is better than the global average on the New Eurasian and China–Indochina corridors.

• On trade facilitation benchmarks, including Doing Business and the Logistics Performance Index, only two of the six land corridors rank in the top half of countries globally (the New Eurasian and China–Indochina corridors); and three of the six rank below the global average on all benchmarks (China–Pakistan, China–Mongolia–Russia, and China–Central Asia–West Asia).

Beyond this overall weak performance is the wide variation. For example, within the New Eurasian Corridor, the Czech Republic ranks 19th in the world on customs performance on the Logistics Performance Index, while Belarus ranks 112th. With supply chains only as strong as their weakest link, and a premium on timeliness and reliability, wide gaps in trade facilitation could undermine the potential benefit of the BRI corridors in unlocking new trade opportunities. This is especially important for increasing the role of corridor economies in global value chains.

**Figure 1.13:** Average time to comply with import and export requirements, by BRI corridor

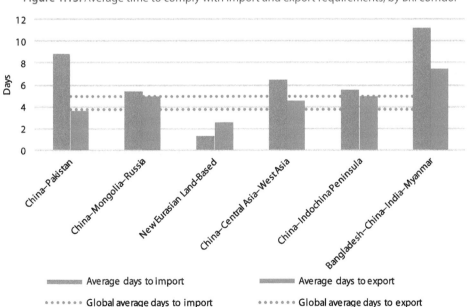

*Source:* Bartley Johns et al. 2018 based on *Doing Business* 2018.

## Tariffs and nontariff barriers

Despite broad and major declines in tariffs over time, liberalization has slowed in recent years, and tariffs remain uneven across regions. In addition, nontariff barriers have in some cases proliferated, and some countries resort to para-tariffs (taxes levied on imports but not on domestic output) or other creative tariffs.[15]

Tariffs in Belt and Road corridor economies, though lower than decades ago, are still above the average for G7 countries and vary widely by region (figure 1.14). The average tariff of corridor economies in Sub-Saharan Africa is twice that of corridor economies in East Asia and Pacific and three times that of the G7. This is true regardless of the use of different forms of country-specific tariff averages, including simple and weighted averages. The Overall Trade Restrictiveness Indicator (OTRI), a more inclusive measure of trade policy, points to even higher protectionism than tariffs alone suggest. This is because OTRI accounts for nontariff barriers in addition to tariffs. The regional patterns of OTRI are also slightly different, with corridor economies in Europe and Central Asia exhibiting lower values than those in East Asia and Pacific and G7.

**Figure 1.14:** Tariffs and the Overall Trade Restrictiveness Indicator in Belt and Road corridor economies and G7 countries, 2016

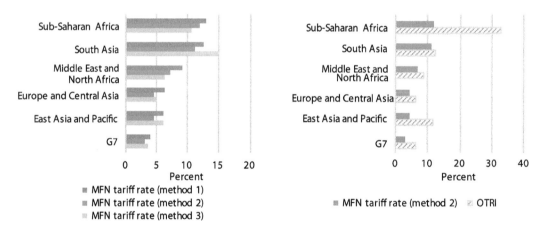

*Source:* UNCTAD Trade Analysis and Information System, World Integrated Trade Solutions (TRAINS-WITS), and OTRI database.

*Note:* Tariffs for prior years are used when those for 2016 are not available. Method 1 is the simple average of country tariff rates, where the latter are computed for each country as the simple average of the country's 6-digit-level tariff rates. Method 2 is the simple average of country tariff rates, where the latter are computed for each country as the weighted average of the country's 6-digit-level tariff rates, with weights given by the country's 6-digit-level import values. Method 3 is the simple average of country tariff rates, where the latter are computed for each country as the weighted average of the country's 6-digit-level tariff rates, with weights given by the world's 6-digit-level import values. The Overall Trade Restrictiveness Index refers to the year 2010 MFN = most-favored nation.

[15] See World Bank (2018a) for an analysis of para-tariffs in South Asia.

## Restrictions on FDI

FDI policy is generally more restrictive in Belt and Road corridor economies than in high-income countries (Chen and Lin 2018). Corridor economies impose on average more restrictions and burdens than high-income OECD countries on starting a foreign business, accessing industrial land, and arbitrating commercial disputes (figure 1.15). For example, the index for the ease of starting a foreign business is around 80 (of 100) in high-income OECD countries but around 70 in corridor economies. Corridor economies are on average more restrictive on foreign ownership than non-Belt and Road and high-income OECD countries. Services such as construction, tourism, retail, media, banking, insurance, and telecom tend to see more restrictions in corridor economies than in non-Belt and Road and high-income OECD countries. And in a comparison of the top 10 and bottom 10 corridor economies, it takes around 16 days to lease land in the Philippines but more than 259 days in Afghanistan. Georgia opens all its sectors to foreign investment, scoring 100 on the openness index, while Thailand scores 52.

## Trade agreements

The number of trade agreements of Belt and Road corridor economies is comparable to that of non-Belt and Road countries, but corridor economies' agreements are much shallower (table 1.2). Ninety-eight separate agreements involve at least two corridor economies, while 115 are between Belt and Road and non-Belt and Road economies. Agreements between Belt and Road and non-Belt

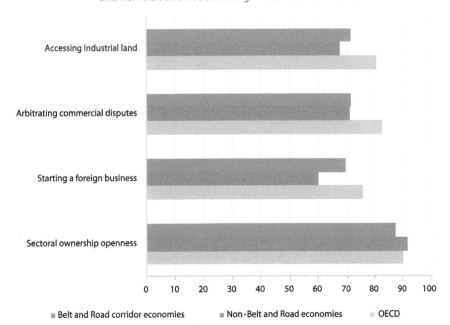

**Figure 1.15:** FDI policy in Belt and Road corridor economies, and non-Belt and Road and high-income OECD countries

*Source:* World Bank, Investing Across Borders, cited in Chen and Lin 2018.

and Road economies, as well as agreements between non–Belt and Road countries, tend to include a larger number of large number of provisions—especially World Trade Organization (WTO) "Extra" provisions, which are outside the WTO mandate. Specifically, corridor economies' agreements with non–Belt and Road countries often include provisions about movement of capital, investment, intellectual property rights protection, and environmental laws, which are seldom included in agreements between corridor economies.

Deepening commitments among corridor economies involves at least two dimensions. A first dimension concerns the coverage of more areas. Some policy areas already covered

**Table 1.2:** Frequency of provision coverage in trade agreements

| | | Belt and Road economies with Belt and Road economies (*N*=98) | Belt and Road economies with non–Belt and Road economies (*N*=115) | Non–Belt and Road economies with non–Belt and Road economies (*N*=110) |
|---|---|---|---|---|
| **WTO Plus** | Tariffs on manufacturing goods | 100 | 100 | 100 |
| | Tariffs on agricultural goods | 99 | 100 | 100 |
| | Customs | 91 | 97 | 94 |
| | Anti-dumping | 59 | 95 | 84 |
| | Export taxes | 80 | 83 | 90 |
| | Countervailing measures | 46 | 85 | 74 |
| | Technical barriers to trade | 50 | 81 | 85 |
| | General Agreement on Trade in Services | 45 | 72 | 83 |
| | Sanitary and phytosanitary measures | 48 | 73 | 80 |
| | State aid | 57 | 78 | 75 |
| | Trade-Related Aspects of Intellectual Property Rights | 43 | 77 | 62 |
| | Public procurement | 39 | 67 | 75 |
| | State trading enterprises | 43 | 57 | 65 |
| | Trade-related investment measures | 18 | 36 | 45 |
| **WTO Extra** | Competition policy | 77 | 81 | 83 |
| | Movement of capital | 37 | 64 | 75 |
| | Investment | 26 | 65 | 74 |
| | Intellectual property rights | 32 | 68 | 48 |
| | Environmental laws | 20 | 58 | 63 |
| | Information society | 13 | 38 | 53 |
| | Regional cooperation | 15 | 40 | 47 |
| | Visa and asylum | 20 | 40 | 45 |
| | Agriculture | 29 | 44 | 42 |
| | Research and technology | 23 | 40 | 35 |
| | Labor market regulations | 18 | 37 | 36 |

*Source:* Hofmann, Osnago, and Ruta 2017.
*Note:* The table includes provisions that appear in at least 35 percent of the agreements in each category (Belt and Road corridor with Belt and Road corridor economies, Belt and Road corridor with non–Belt and Road corridor economies, and non–Belt and Road with non–Belt and Road corridor economies).

in agreements with non-BRI partners could be included in agreements between corridor economies (see table 1.2). Among the WTO Plus provisions (which are under the WTO mandate), technical barriers to trade, sanitary and phytosanitary measures, and public procurement are important areas that are usually missing from agreements between corridor economies. So are other important policy areas such as the regulation of capital movement and restrictions on foreign direct investment. The second dimension concerns the fragmentation of rules. The 98 trade agreements among corridor economies contribute to create different trade rules. Having a fragmented set of rules could inhibit the emergence of regional supply chains by increasing the costs of cross-border production, such as the costs of complying with different standards.

## 1.3 THE BRI'S COST AND FINANCING

### *What is the cost of the BRI?*

Popular estimates for Chinese investment under the BRI range from US$1 trillion to US$8 trillion (Hillman 2018). The wide range in part reflects the undefined scope of the initiative, but also the limited data availability on the number, size, and terms of the projects.

This study used different approaches to quantify the costs of the BRI. For 70 Belt and Road corridor economies (excluding China), the World Bank estimates that BRI investment is worth US$575 billion. This includes projects in all sectors, not only transport, that are already executed, in implementation phase, and planned (Bandiera and Tsiropoulos 2019).[16] Ideally, the BRI costs for governments could be identified by public and publicly guaranteed debt-financing related to BRI projects. A comparison with data on Chinese loan commitments in corridor economies from the World Bank's Debtor Reporting System (DRS) shows a small difference in the investment data at the aggregate level, but also points to large discrepancies for some countries.[17] These estimates do not factor in the typical risks of megaprojects, which could push costs substantially higher than initially planned (see box 4.1 in chapter 4).

The largest BRI investments are in energy (figure 1.16). Total investment in transport infrastructure, the focus of this study, is estimated to be US$144 billion in the 70 corridor economies. The energy and transport industries absorb 71 percent of the total costs of the BRI. Two-thirds of the identified financing is expected to be to countries in East Asia and Pacific

---

[16] Investment financing has been compiled by WIND, a Chinese consultancy company, for the World Bank. The database covers both China's global investment and construction contacts; outward investment in nonfinancial sectors; and projects that are completed, under construction, or planned. The planned ones are all officially confirmed projects.

[17] The comparison is limited to 24 of 43 countries with identified BRI investment either planned or under construction during 2013–17. It differs by around US$10 billion with respect to the investment data.

and Europe and Central Asia, with the remainder mainly to South Asia and the Middle East and North Africa, and only 2 percent to Sub-Saharan Africa. Almost all expected financing will be to lower- and upper-middle-income countries, with only 1 percent to low-income countries and 11 percent to high-income economies (see figure 1.16). A large share of this investment, US$525 billion or 91 percent, is expected to be received by International Bank for Reconstruction and Development– or International Development Association–eligible countries. Only US$66 billion went to projects already completed by the end of 2016; most BRI investment is on projects in the construction or planning phase.

**Figure 1.16:** BRI investments in Belt and Road corridor economies
(Percentage shares of US$575 billion)

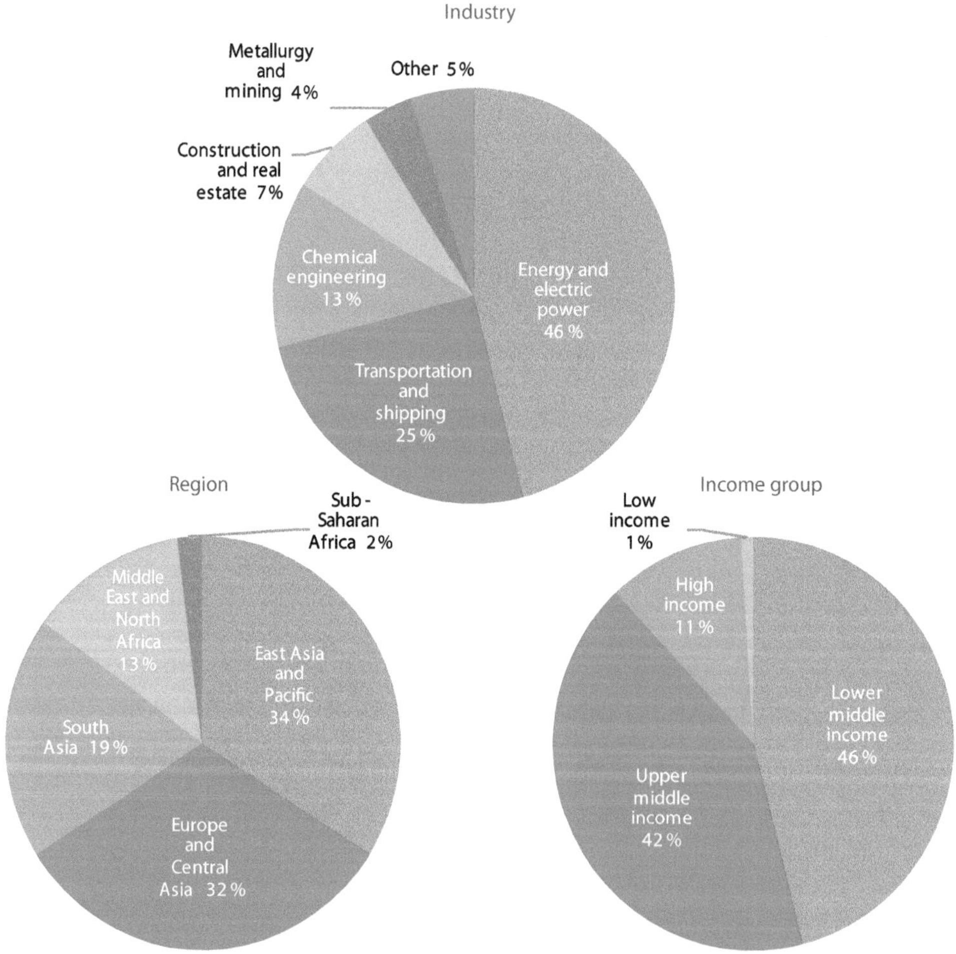

Industry

- Metallurgy and mining 4%
- Other 5%
- Construction and real estate 7%
- Chemical engineering 13%
- Energy and electric power 46%
- Transportation and shipping 25%

Region

- Sub-Saharan Africa 2%
- Middle East and North Africa 13%
- East Asia and Pacific 34%
- South Asia 19%
- Europe and Central Asia 32%

Income group

- Low income 1%
- High income 11%
- Lower middle income 46%
- Upper middle income 42%

*Source:* Bandiera and Tsiropoulos 2019.

**Figure 1.17:** Bottom-up costs of BRI transport infrastructure investments
(Percentage shares of US$368 billion)

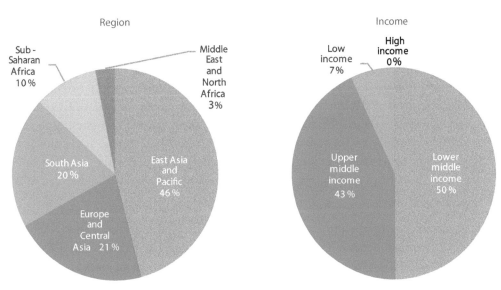

*Source:* de Soyres, Mulabdic, and Ruta 2019.

The total cost of BRI transport infrastructure investments related to rail and port projects for 70 corridor economies increases to US$304 billion if a bottom-up approach is used (de Soyres, Mulabdic, and Ruta 2019).[18] The costs of the BRI infrastructure projects in appendix B were computed by combining information from World Bank country teams, which draw on publicly available sources on the costs of a small subset of BRI projects, and assumptions about construction costs per kilometer of new rail junctions and improvements of existing rails, tunnels, canals, and bridges. The different figures mostly reflect the diverse criteria to identify BRI projects. Despite these differences, the data show that the geographical distribution of infrastructure costs resembles the one for the overall BRI investment. The exception is Sub-Saharan Africa, which is expected to incur a higher share of the total BRI costs (figure 1.17). Similarly, this difference is reflected in the cost shares by income, with low-income economies expected to bear 7 percent of the total costs of infrastructure.

### BRI financing

The BRI takes place in the context of rapidly rising public and corporate debt. Public debt in emerging market economies (EMEs) has been rising, reaching levels not seen since the 1980s. It has been accompanied by changes in public debt composition and by rising corporate debt in EMEs, now exceeding historic levels and adding to fiscal risks and vulnerabilities. Similarly, debt risks in low-income

---

[18] The cost of BRI transport projects in China is estimated to be an additional US$64 billion.

developing countries (LIDCs) have risen substantially in recent years. The share of countries at high risk of debt distress or in debt distress has doubled since 2013—to about 40 percent.

Expected BRI investments are very large for some countries. Some 66 percent of the total BRI investment is expected to accrue to seven countries, with Indonesia, Malaysia, Pakistan, and the Russian Federation accounting for 50 percent of the total. Scaled by 2017 GDP, the median BRI investment amounts to under 6 percent of GDP, an amount that is not large in relation to the investment needs of many countries, especially if disbursed over several years. For example, median annual BRI financing in the WIND database would amount to slightly more than 1 percent of GDP if disbursed over the five years until 2023. But in some countries estimated investment surpasses 20 percent of 2017 GDP (figure 1.18).

BRI investment takes place in countries with very different debt sustainability situations. Since 2012, median debt-to-GDP ratios have increased for LIDCs and EMEs. This trend affects countries receiving BRI investments at rates similar to non-Belt and Road economies (figures 1.19 and 1.20). One-third of BRI-recipient LIDCs with a recent debt sustainability analysis, have a high risk of debt distress. Nearly two-thirds of BRI-recipient EMEs face elevated debt vulnerabilities, requiring high scrutiny, with debt above the indicative thresholds of 50 percent of GDP or gross financing needs above 15 percent of GDP. Countries with already vulnerable debt situations may have very limited fiscal space to take on new borrowing.

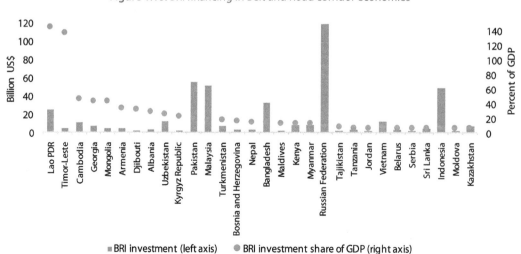

**Figure 1.18:** BRI financing in Belt and Road corridor economies

*Source:* WIND database and *World Development Indicators.*

**Figure 1.19:** General government gross debt
(Percent of GDP)

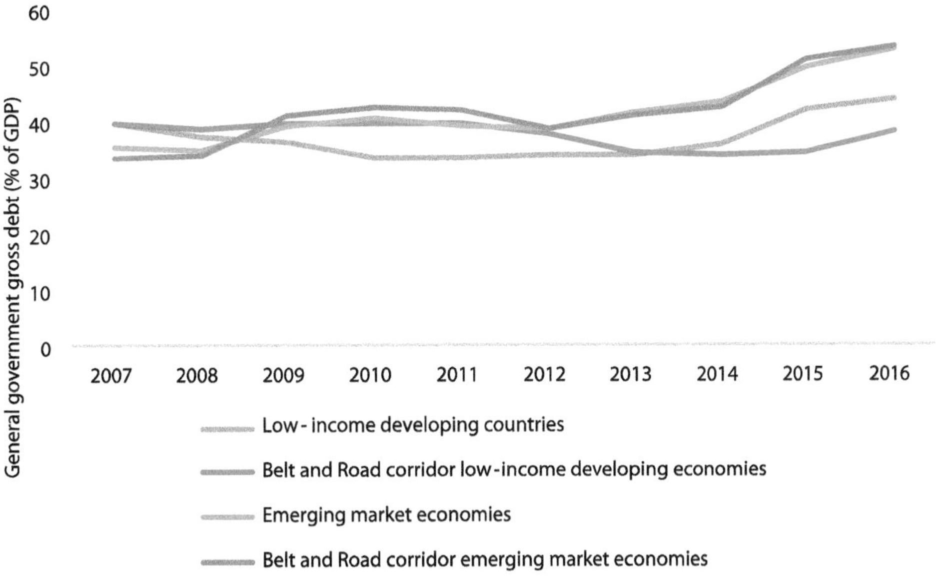

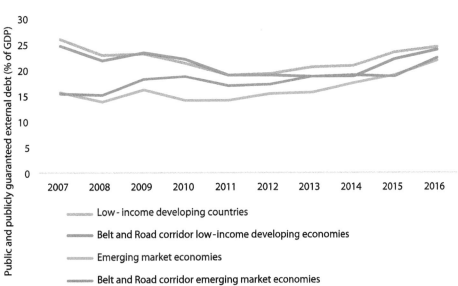

*Source:* International Debt Statistics.

**Figure 1.20:** Public and publicly guaranteed external debt
(Median levels, percent of GDP)

*Source:* World Bank and International Monetary Fund debt sustainability analyses.

External debt from non–Paris Club countries, including China, is historically small in corridor economies. But it has increased in countries at higher risk of debt distress, particularly LIDCs. Debt from multilateral and traditional bilateral creditors represented more than 70 percent of all external public debt of BRI-recipient LIDCs in 2016. Consistent with the general trend of increased debt vulnerabilities in LIDCs, the group of BRI-recipient LIDCs has over time increased reliance on private financing, including bonds and bank financing, doubling in the past 10 years. Nonconcessional financing has increased especially in those BRI LIDCs with moderate risk of debt distress. Exposure to non–Paris Club official creditors, including China, has also increased for the BRI LIDCs, reaching 22 percent of total external public debt. The largest increase in exposure to nontraditional creditors was in LIDCs with moderate and high risk of debt distress, with most of the increase in the latter group due to large borrowing by Lao PDR (figure 1.21).

**Figure 1.21:** Debt composition of BRI-recipient low-income developing countries
(Percent of total)

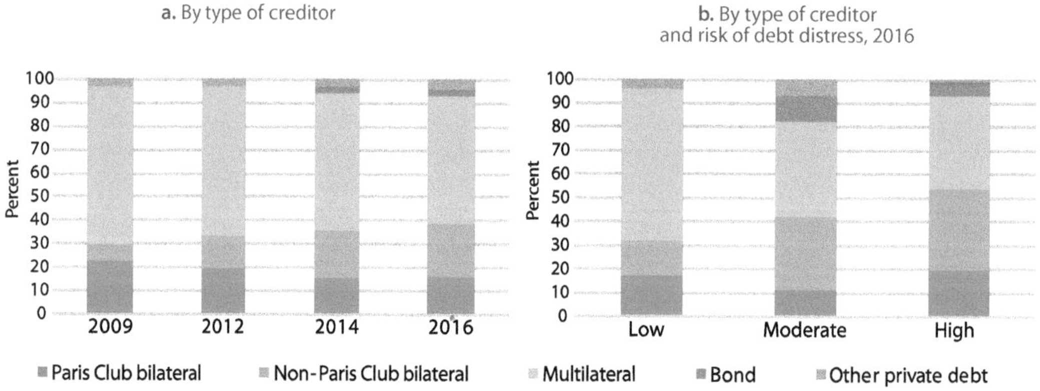

a. By type of creditor

b. By type of creditor and risk of debt distress, 2016

■ Paris Club bilateral   ■ Non-Paris Club bilateral   ▧ Multilateral   ■ Bond   ▧ Other private debt

*Source:* Bandiera and Tsiropoulos 2019.

# CHAPTER 2

Economic effects of BRI
transport infrastructure

New BRI investments in transport could boost the real economies of participating countries and the global economy overall. Across a range of dimensions, the impact of BRI investments is expected to be positive, but not for all countries. The improved transport network is expected to reduce trade times and costs and to increase overall trade as Belt and Road corridor economies increase exports and diversify their production. This expansion will increase trade both between corridor economies and to non-Belt and Road countries as market access opens. The decline in trade times will also increase foreign direct investment, especially for lower-income countries. The increased trade and investment will boost GDP and welfare, thus reducing poverty in the region.[1] While the improved transportation network leads to aggregate gains, individual projects may still fail, and individual countries may lose due to the high cost of infrastructure relative to trade gains.

## 2.1 HOW MUCH WILL BRI TRANSPORT INFRASTRUCTURE PROJECTS REDUCE TRADE COSTS?

BRI projects—rails, roads, ports, and the like—will build on the existing network of transport infrastructure, creating new links and making the network denser. Information on the existing network is reasonably good, but compiling a list of transport infrastructure projects associated with the BRI is a delicate task since there is no official list and no one criterion defines what is—or is not—part of the initiative. Indeed, there might be projects financed by loans from China that do not necessarily fall under the BRI, and there might be projects with non-Chinese financing that are still considered part of it.

The BRI transport infrastructure projects in this study are identified by two criteria (Reed and Trubetskoy 2019). First, the project is located along the overland corridors forming the "Belt" or along the "Road" in one of the 71 economies analyzed in this study. Second, the project is explicitly mentioned as part of the BRI in an official document, by a government official, or in an article by a major academic journal or news source. For some analyses, the focus is on projects affecting travel between major cities (with at least 300,000 inhabitants). These criteria present the advantage of restricting the list to projects related to the BRI and—for analytical tractability—excluding some projects that are not connecting major cities. To ensure consistency with information on the ground, the study team validated it with the help of World Bank country offices.

The full set of BRI-related transport projects considered in this study is in figure 2.1 (details are in appendix B). It neither is an official nor an exhaustive list of Belt and

---

[1] The focus here is on the impact of the improved transport network on economic activity through trade and FDI. As Gould (2018) discussed, improvements in transport, trade, and FDI can also affect other dimensions of connectivity such as migration and knowledge transfers that can further contribute to improvements in economic activity.

**Figure 2.1:** BRI-related transport projects

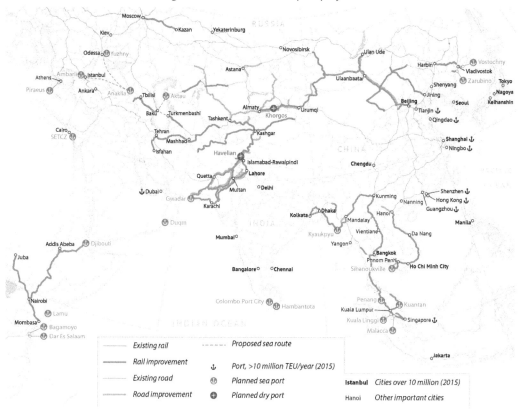

*Source:* Reed and Trubetskoy 2019.
*Note:* TEU = twenty-foot equivalent unit.

Road transport infrastructure, and, indeed, other lists have been compiled elsewhere using different criteria.[2] The status of these projects also differs widely (appendix B). Some have been completed, with the infrastructure already operational, such as with the Central Rail Corridor connecting China, Mongolia, and the Russian Federation. Other projects—such as the railway connecting Aktau in Kazakhstan with Khorgos at the border with China—are under construction, and implementation stages vary widely. Still other projects, such as the Kra Canal in Thailand, are uncertain. And as the BRI progresses, additional projects not currently considered by the authorities (and thus not in this study) will add to the list of BRI infrastructure.

The BRI is not happening in isolation and, indeed, several regional infrastructure initiatives are also in varying stages of implementation. The Greater Mekong Subregion

---

[2] An alternative source is the database compiled by Reconnecting Asia at the Center for Strategic and International Studies, which includes transportation projects (roads, rails, ports, bridges, and tunnels) as well as other elements such as electrifying special economic zones in Asia.

**Box 2.1:** The European Union's TEN-T and its extension to Eastern Europe

At the beginning of the 1990s, the European Union member states decided to set up an infrastructure policy to support the functioning of the internal market through integrated and efficient transport, energy, and telecommunications networks. The Trans-European Transport Network (TEN-T) is directed toward implementing and developing a Europe-wide network of roads, railway lines, inland waterways, maritime shipping routes, ports, airports, and railroad terminals. The policy encompasses building new physical infrastructure; adopting innovative digital technologies, alternative fuels, and universal standards; and modernizing and upgrading existing infrastructure and platforms.

TEN-T identifies nine Core Network Corridors spanning the entire European Union for coordinated development. Motorways of the Sea, the maritime pillar of the TEN-T, connects Core Network Corridors through maritime links, complemented by the European Railway Traffic Management System, which aims to enhance cross-border interoperability, creating a seamless, Europe-wide rail system.

In November 2017, the European Union, its member states, and its six Eastern neighbors in the Eastern Partnership—Armenia, Azerbaijan, Belarus, Georgia, Moldova, and Ukraine—endorsed the extension of TEN-T to Eastern Europe. An investment action plan was prepared to assist decisionmakers in prioritizing strategic investments in transport infrastructure with the aim of expanding the TEN-T network (World Bank 2018b). The plan identified priority investments of around 12.8 billion euros up to 2030. The priorities have been developed by combining a continued consultation process with a multicriteria assessment and taking into account strategic fit, economic viability, and environmental and social factors.

(GMS) is an initiative launched in 1992 by six countries in the Mekong River region (Cambodia, China, Lao PDR, Myanmar, Thailand, and Vietnam). The GMS program aims to enhance economic cooperation among its members through cross-border infrastructure development. Other regional initiatives that corridor economies are participating in include the Central Asia Regional Economic Cooperation program, which includes 10 Central Asian countries as well as China, and the ASEAN Master Plan for Connectivity, which includes the 10 members of the Association of South East Asian Nations. Several countries have announced bilateral infrastructure initiatives, including Japan, the Republic of Korea, the Russian Federation, and the European Union (box 2.1). Japan's Expanded Partnership for Quality Infrastructure, for example, aims to disburse about $200 billion to infrastructure projects in 2016–21.[3] These regional infrastructure initiatives are outside the scope of this analysis. But they will affect the transport network of corridor economies, pointing to the need to coordinate financing and project development in the region.

---

[3] The announcement can be found here: https://www.meti.go.jp/english/press/2016/0523_01.html.

## *Quantifying the BRI's impact on shipment times and trade costs*

The methodology to quantify how much the BRI will reduce shipment times and trade costs is based on two steps (de Soyres et al. 2018).

- First, it uses a combination of geographical data and network algorithms to compute the reduction in travel times between 1,000 cities in 191 countries. As a starting point, the global network of railways and ports in 2013 is used to estimate the pre-BRI shipment times between every pair of cities. From this reference point, an "improved scenario" enriches the transportation network with planned infrastructure projects (see figure 2.1). Comparing the before and after scenarios allows quantifying the changes in shipment times induced by the new and improved transport infrastructure projects.

- Second, sectoral estimates of "value of time" transform reductions in shipment time into reductions in trade costs.[4] Different goods have different values of time. For instance, fresh fruits are perishable and are very time-sensitive; microchips need to be delivered to producers just in time. So, the value of time needs to be computed for each pair of countries and each sector. These country pair–sector values of time can be further aggregated to quantify changes in trade costs by country.

Using these methods, new data are produced on shipment times and trade costs for Belt and Road corridor and non–Belt and Road economies.[5] Comparing before and after outcomes allows quantifying the impact of the Belt and Road Initiative on shipment times and trade costs. The analysis does not assume that all infrastructure is good. Instead, it lets the data decide by estimating the effects on travel times and trade costs of the network of BRI-related projects.[6]

The initiative can reduce shipment times for corridor economies, particularly along economic corridors. Corridor economies can on average experience a 3.2 percent reduction in shipment times with the rest of the world and 4 percent with other corridor economies. Along individual economic corridors shipment times come down on average by 8.5 percent and by as much as 12 percent (figure 2.2). The largest estimated gains are for the trade routes connecting East and South Asia and along the corridors that are part of the BRI. For instance, shipment times between countries in the China–Central Asia–West Asia economic corridor decline from an average of 15 days before the BRI to 13 days once the infrastructure projects are completed and operational.

---

[4] These estimates come from Hummels and Schaur 2013.

[5] The data can be accessed at https://datacatalog.worldbank.org/dataset/bri-trade-costs-database-wps8614-0.

[6] Individually, some infrastructure is estimated to be of little value, leading to a risk of stranded infrastructure (see box 2.2).

**Figure 2.2:** Average reduction in shipping times by economy

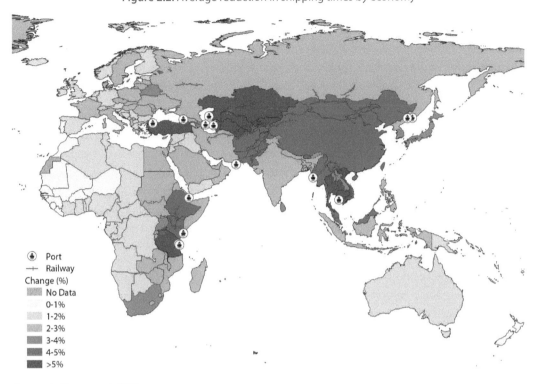

*Source:* de Soyres et al. 2018.
*Note:* For each economy, the aggregate proportional decline is computed as the average of the proportional shipping time decline with all other economies in the world.

Reduced shipping times substantially reduce trade costs. Implementing all BRI transport infrastructure projects would reduce aggregate trade costs for the corridor economies with the rest of the world by 2.8 percent on average and with other corridor economies by 3.5 percent. For shipment times, the reductions in trade costs vary widely across pairs of countries—with East Asia and Pacific as well as South Asia having the largest average reductions. Similarly, trade costs will fall more along corridors. For instance, trade costs along the China–Central Asia–West Asia economic corridor would decline by 10 percent.

The Belt and Road Initiative can have positive spillovers on shipment times and trade costs of non-Belt and Road economies. The average decline in travel times across all country pairs in the world is 2.5 percent, and that of trade costs is 2.2 percent. The reason is that non-Belt and Road economies may benefit from the improved network of BRI infrastructure. For example, Tanzania's Bagamoyo port is expected to benefit not only Tanzania but several other countries in Sub-Saharan Africa. As a result, when all BRI transport projects are implemented, the shipment time between Australia and Rwanda is expected to come down by 0.5 percent. Similarly, improving Djibouti's port will contribute to a 1.2 percent decline in the shipment time between Australia and Ethiopia.

## *Considering a subset of BRI projects*

Different BRI transport projects have different feasibilities, which may affect their likelihood of being completed. To account for the uncertainty surrounding specific projects, the methods just discussed are applied only to the subset of projects that have moved beyond the planning stage and are currently operational or under construction—excluding those classified in appendix B as "proposed," "postponed," or "cancelled."

Comparing the results with the full list of BRI projects and with the revised list provides some insights. Changes in trade times and trade costs are smaller if a subset of transportation projects is implemented. This is particularly true for Belt and Road corridor economies, but it also applies to the positive spillover effect that BRI projects can have on trade costs of non-Belt and Road economies. Average trade costs of corridor economies would decline by 2.2 percent (down from 2.8 percent), and trade costs for the world by 1.8 percent (down from 2.2 percent).

While differences do not appear to be very large at the aggregate level, they can be more significant for some regions and countries. Trade costs for East Asia and Pacific economies would decline the most from implementing the full set of projects. Completing only a subset of projects would deliver reductions in trade costs that are half those in the full list. Most affected by partially implementing projects among corridor economies would be Cambodia (3.7 percent point loss), Thailand (2.7 percent), and Vietnam (3.1 percent). Several economies in other regions would lower their trade cost gain from a less dense network of transportation infrastructure, though the changes are less pronounced than for East Asian economies.

---

**Box 2.2:** Successful BRI projects and the risk of stranded infrastructure

Will Belt and Road corridor economies stand to gain substantially from connectivity-enhancing improvements, or will they be stuck with stranded infrastructure? The value of the transport infrastructure created is not the cost of the concrete poured but the additional market access and potential indirect or wider economic benefits that the connection provides. These benefits take time to materialize, so defining success or failure at an early stage is difficult. Keeping this in mind, this box assesses the value of individual Belt and Road Initiative (BRI) transport projects for market access and discusses two recently completed BRI projects, the port of Piraeus and the Khorgos–Almaty road, that have reduced travel times and improved connectivity.

### Market access value for individual BRI transport projects

Several transport infrastructure projects have been widely discussed in the press, either because they failed to attract shipping (Hambantota port in Sri Lanka) or because they were scaled down by the host country's government (Kyaupyu Port in Myanmar) or renegotiated to reduce costs (East Coast Rail Link in Malaysia). Which projects are likely to create stranded assets? A proper appraisal of individual BRI transport projects is beyond the scope of this study, but a gravity model allows identifying some characteristics that make individual investment more likely to be (un)successful.

Using this approach, Reed and Trubetskoy (2019) assessed the value of 68 BRI projects. Half of them generate little value when built in isolation because they connect only smaller cities or do not add new least-cost paths between cities. But when the entire network of projects is built, the share falls to around one-third, confirming that the value of each project depends on other projects. The most valuable projects connect highly populous cities to the network, such as the Kunming–Kolkata High Speed Rail (Bangladesh, India, and Myanmar), the Tehran–Mashhad rail electrification in the Islamic Republic of Iran, and the expansion of the ML-1 Karachi–Hyderabad–Lahore–Peshawar railway in Pakistan. This analysis points to the importance of project selection and appraisal to ensure the success of BRI investment.

### Two success stories: The Port of Piraeus and the Khorgos–Almaty Road

The Greek port of Piraeus has two terminals handling containers: Terminal I (Pier I) and Terminal II (Pier II and Pier III). Terminal I, with a capacity of 1 million twenty-foot equivalent units (TEU), is operated by the Piraeus Port Authority, which has been majority owned by China COSCO Shipping Group since August 2016. Terminal II is run by COSCO Pacific under a 35-year concession signed in 2008. The agreement between Piraeus Port Authority and COSCO allowed investment not only in new piers, but also in a rail link between the port's terminals and the national rail system (Arvis et al. 2019). COSCO is a conglomerate of companies involved in maritime transport and logistics, which includes a container shipping line and one of the largest container-terminal operators.

In 2016, Piraeus annual container throughput reached 3.7 million TEU, which represents a 168 percent increase in 2007–16. In 2007, Piraeus was not among the top 15 container ports in Europe, but in 2016 it ranked as the 8th largest container port on the continent (Notteboom 2017). This impressive increase has been largely driven by growth in transshipment, likely relocations from other transshipment ports. Thanks to the performance gains at Piraeus, Greece has seen a significant connectivity boost (Arvis et al. 2019). Greece's Liner Shipping Connectivity Index increased from 27 in 2008 to 59 in 2018.

The Khorgos–Almaty road along the New Eurasian Land Bridge Corridor was recently upgraded. The road connects Khorgos, the primary road border crossing point between Kazakhstan and China, with Almaty, one of the major economic centers of Central Asia. The project upgraded the 305 kilometers of road between Khorgos and Almaty from a two-lane to a four-lane highway. This section completed the improvement of the corridor between Urumqi (China) and Yaysan (Kazakhstan) on the border with Russia.

The road improvement, completed in 2018, has already reduced travel times and transport costs. By June 2018, transport costs between Khorgos and Almaty had declined from US$0.26 to US$0.24 per vehicle-kilometer, and travel times had fallen by 40 percent, from five hours to three. The reduced transport costs and travel times are expected to trigger increased trade in the coming years.

## 2.2 IMPACT ON TRADE AND FOREIGN INVESTMENT

As a first step in the economic analysis of the Belt and Road Initiative, this section focuses on the impact of BRI transport infrastructure projects on trade and investment flows. The key questions are how the denser network of transport infrastructure will affect world trade, trade between Belt and Road corridor economies, and their inflows of FDI. The analysis uses the data on the impact of the BRI on shipment times and trade costs presented in the previous section as input into three modeling approaches: computable general equilibrium (CGE), structural general equilibrium (SGE), and gravity models.[7] The diverse approaches allow different perspectives on the effects of the Belt and Road Initiative, thus offering a more robust quantification of the projected outcomes.

### *Trade*

### Overall trade flows

Transport infrastructure related to the Belt and Road Initiative is expected to boost world trade (figure 2.3). Results from the CGE model show that the volume of global exports increases by 1.7 percent (in 2030 relative to the baseline).[8] World trade growth is driven by Belt and Road corridor economies' exports, which increase by 2.8 percent. BRI transport infrastructure will also have a positive effect on exports of non–Belt and Road economies in aggregate, because BRI transport projects will reduce trade costs of non–Belt and Road corridor economies as their exporters take advantage of the denser transport network. The non–Belt and Road corridor economies show an increase in exports of 0.7 percent. Among non–Belt and Road corridor economies, countries like Ethiopia, which benefit from the better connection of the new ports in East Africa, have the largest trade gains. Other large effects are for the United States and for high-income countries in East Asia. But not all non–Belt and Road economies benefit in trade growth, with slight decreases in Latin America and Rest of Western Europe due to trade diversion.

The trade impact of BRI transport projects is positive for all corridor economies, with sizable differences. The reduction in trade costs associated with new transport infrastructure allows firms in corridor economies to connect better to markets and regional and global value chains,

---

[7] The computable general equilibrium (CGE) results are from Maliszewska and van der Mensbrugghe (2019). They are based on the ENVISAGE model which is a global, recursive dynamic CGE model developed at the World Bank. The model incorporates five different production factors, includes 28 sectors, and comprises 34 countries and regions. The CGE results are complemented with estimates from a static structural general equilibrium (SGE) model by de Soyres, Mulabdic and Ruta (2019). This is based on Caliendo and Parro (2015)—a Ricardian model with sectoral linkages, trade in intermediate goods, and sectoral heterogeneity—which allows including 107 countries and regions. The effects of the BRI on trade between corridor economies and on FDI flows to these countries are investigated with a standard gravity model. This is a partial equilibrium approach, which does not account for the effects of BRI infrastructure on the economy as a whole, but it allows including all corridor economies and highly disaggregated sectors in the analysis. Results are from Baniya, Rocha, and Ruta (2018) and Chen and Lin (2018).

[8] New technologies such as 3D printing have been accompanied by predictions of a future world where global supply chains will be shortened, and international trade will be dramatically reduced, potentially making transport infrastructure less relevant. While the analysis for this report abstracts from the impact of new technologies on trade flows, recent research finds that international trade has actually increased as a result of the adoption of 3D printing (Freund, Mulabdic, and Ruta 2019).

**Figure 2.3:** BRI infrastructure improvements will increase exports (CGE and SGE models)

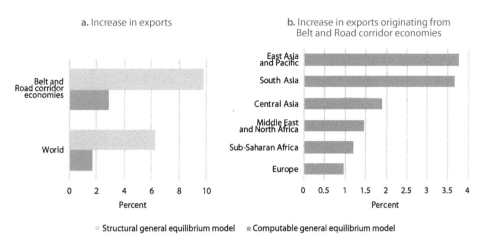

**a.** Increase in exports

**b.** Increase in exports originating from Belt and Road corridor economies

▪ Structural general equilibrium model ▪ Computable general equilibrium model

*Sources:* Maliszewska and van der Mensbrugghe 2019; de Soyres, Mulabdic, and Ruta 2019.

importing cheaper and higher quality inputs, thus increasing productivity and the ability to export. Total exports of the East Asia and Pacific and South Asia regions increase respectively by 3.8 and 3.7 percent. The largest percentage increases in exports include Thailand (14.9 percent), Malaysia (12.4 percent), Pakistan (9.8 percent), and Bangladesh (8.7 percent). Total exports from the Middle East and North Africa, Central Asia, and the corridor economies in Sub-Saharan Africa increase by 2.0, 1.9, and 1.2 percent, respectively. The smallest gains are for Eastern Europe whose exports increase by 0.2 percent, with some countries such as Poland experiencing a slight reduction in exports because the new infrastructure reduces their competitiveness relative to other economies.

The trade effects of the BRI transport infrastructure predicted by the structural model tend to be larger (figure 2.3). World export volumes increase by 6.3 percent. Corridor economies are expected to increase exports by almost 10 percent. Similar to the CGE results, the increase in non-Belt and Road economies' exports is around a third of the increase for corridor economies. The information from the two models should be seen as providing a range of the potential trade effects of the BRI. Different from the CGE analysis, the structural model highlights the linkages through global value chains since it assumes strong complementarities between foreign and domestic inputs in production.[9] As trade costs fall as a result of the denser network of transport infrastructure, the structural model predicts that firms will expand their use of imported inputs more, with larger effects on their productivity and exports. That boosts exports more for low- and upper-middle-income corridor economies.

---

[9] Technically, the two models assume different production functions and different trade elasticities. Other factors also explain the larger trade effects in the structural model. The CGE model has a more detailed structure of the economy, which allows more thorough investigation of the sectoral and dynamic effects. The larger disaggregation in the structural model allows capturing the impact of lower trade costs associated with BRI transport projects on trade flows for a larger number of countries. These intraregional effects appear to be quantitatively relevant as most country-pairs in the world will experience a decrease in trade cost due to the BRI transport projects. This effect is magnified when there are important complementarities between foreign and domestic inputs in production and larger trade elasticities, as assumed by the structural model.

## Bilateral trade flows

The BRI is expected to reshape trade relations for participating economies with each other and with the rest of the world. Long trading times before the BRI kept intraregional trade low for these economies (chapter 1). The three models predict that BRI transport infrastructure projects will increase intra-BRI trade substantially, between 4.1 and 7.2 percent.

All regions expand their exports to East Asia and Pacific, reflecting the large increase in imports by China (5.6 percent) and, to less extent, by other economies in the region with high manufacturing import growth such as Thailand (table 2.1). The improved connectivity will also allow East Asia and Pacific economies to expand their exports among themselves and to other regions, most notably the Middle East and North Africa and Sub-Saharan Africa-reflecting intensifying regional value chains. Other large changes in bilateral flows include the increased trade within Central Asia, now poorly connected to itself, and exports from the Sub-Saharan corridor economies to most other regions. The new infrastructure will allow South Asia to increase its exports to East Asia, but most of its export growth will be toward non-Belt and Road economies, boosting global integration.

## Sectoral trade flows

The reduction in trading times associated with BRI transport projects will affect exports of different goods differently depending on their time-sensitivity. Results from the gravity analysis suggest that the BRI will more strongly increase trade in such perishable products as fresh fruits and vegetable, livestock, nuts, and crops that will benefit the most from the ability to transport final products to consumers or end users on time (Baniya, Rocha, and Ruta 2018). But exporters will also benefit from the ability to import time-sensitive inputs more quickly. Indeed, the specialization in exports such as meat products, chemicals, rubber and plastics, and electronics will increase, given the ability to access intermediate inputs on time, suggesting the importance of new infrastructure for global and regional value chains in corridor economies.

The BRI will also change the comparative advantage of countries and regions. As trade costs are lowered due to reductions in shipping times, countries would tend to specialize in trade of time-

**Table 2.1:** Changes in trade among Belt and Road corridor economies (CGE model)

| | From BRI to BRI | Central Asia | East Asia and Pacific | Europe | Middle East and North Africa | South Asia | Sub-Saharan Africa | Non-Belt and Road corridor economies |
|---|---|---|---|---|---|---|---|---|
| Exporters | Central Asia | 35.24 | 4.28 | −1.97 | 1.77 | −0.30 | 1.21 | −1.08 |
| | East Asia and Pacific | 1.90 | 6.00 | 3.16 | 10.85 | 3.83 | 7.91 | 2.07 |
| | Europe | −2.37 | 5.37 | −0.60 | 4.50 | 6.03 | 8.29 | −0.79 |
| | Middle East and North Africa | 1.66 | 7.04 | 7.59 | −2.95 | −0.67 | −2.21 | 1.39 |
| | South Asia | −2.32 | 9.35 | 2.92 | −5.06 | −3.20 | −3.55 | 5.15 |
| | Sub-Saharan Africa | 21.20 | 10.98 | −2.68 | −2.06 | 6.30 | 5.59 | −2.17 |

*Source:* Maliszewska and van der Mensbrugghe 2019.

sensitive products or in industries that rely on time-sensitive inputs. Sectoral results from the CGE model point to sizable increases in exports of time-sensitive agricultural products from Central Asia (8.6 percent) and processed foods from Central Asia (17.4 percent) (table 2.2). Exports of sectors that rely on time-sensitive inputs such as chemical products will grow most from the Middle East and North Africa (7.3 percent) and from South Asia (8.3 percent). But the largest increases will be for manufacturing sectors, particularly electronics: exports will increase in East Asia and Pacific (8.3 percent), South Asia (11.8 percent), and the Sub-Saharan corridor economies (6.4 percent). Exports of energy products such as oil and coal will also be affected as well as transport services, particularly from the Middle East and North Africa. This specialization process will imply loss of exports in sectors of comparative disadvantage. The largest reshufflings are for oil exports from East Asia and Pacific and electronics for Europe and Central Asia.

## *Foreign investment*

Longer shipping times constitute a barrier to FDI flows, limiting the ability of countries to trade, thus reducing the value of the location as an export base (see chapter 1). The proposed BRI transport network is expected to lead to a 4.97 percent increase in total FDI flows to Belt and Road corridor economies—a 4.36 percent increase in FDI flows within BRI, a 4.63 percent increase in FDI flows from OECD countries, and a 5.75 percent increase in FDI flows from non–Belt and Road countries.

Across regions, the proposed BRI transport network could increase FDI flows to corridor economies in East Asia and Pacific by 6.3 percent, Europe by 3.7 percent, and Central Asia by 7.3 percent, in the Middle East and North Africa by 3.4 percent, South Asia by 5.2 percent, and Sub-Saharan Africa by 7.5 percent (figure 2.4). Reductions in trading time are estimated to have especially large impacts on low-and lower-middle-income economies— with estimated FDI increases of 7.6 and 6.0 percent respectively.

**Figure 2.4:** Infrastructure improvements are projected to increase foreign direct investment

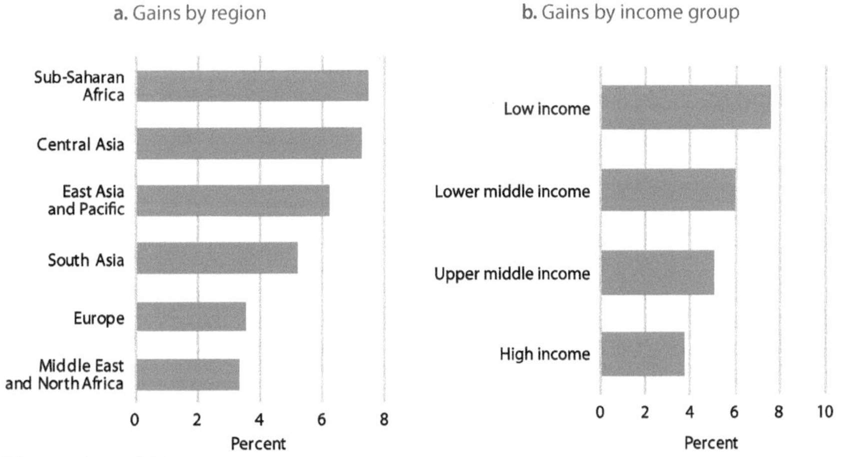

*Source:* Chen and Lin 2018.

**Table 2.2:** Changes in trade among Belt and Road corridor economies (CGE model)

| Sector | Central Asia | East Asia and Pacific | Europe | Middle East and North Africa | South Asia | Sub-Saharan Africa |
|---|---|---|---|---|---|---|
| Agriculture | 8.55 | 0.64 | 3.08 | 2.38 | −2.96 | 2.59 |
| Minerals not elsewhere specified | 0.09 | −1.18 | −0.72 | −0.28 | −0.29 | −1.33 |
| Coal | 2.57 | 1.56 | 5.55 | 38.52 | 1.64 | 13.32 |
| Oil | −1.30 | −8.35 | 0.80 | −0.25 | −4.95 | |
| Gas | 2.73 | −2.35 | 1.48 | 0.94 | 6.53 | |
| Textiles | 5.34 | 1.83 | 1.30 | 0.06 | 2.35 | 0.76 |
| Wearing apparel | 13.58 | 0.66 | 1.52 | −2.29 | 4.52 | 2.20 |
| Leather goods | 38.64 | 2.05 | −0.57 | −2.95 | 0.51 | 8.78 |
| Processed foods | 17.39 | 1.47 | 2.00 | 0.92 | 8.42 | −0.95 |
| Wood products | 16.23 | 2.76 | 2.03 | −3.33 | −3.39 | 3.63 |
| Paper products, publishing | 5.39 | 2.94 | 0.84 | −2.49 | 2.09 | −6.63 |
| Petroleum, coal products | 3.69 | 1.83 | 2.59 | 8.88 | 4.01 | 5.62 |
| Chemicals, rubber, and plastics | 4.02 | 1.27 | 0.72 | 7.25 | 8.27 | −4.33 |
| Energy intensive manufacturing | 2.13 | 1.09 | 0.10 | 0.48 | 3.39 | 4.47 |
| Metal products | 15.79 | 4.58 | 0.66 | −3.66 | 6.43 | −1.52 |
| Electronics | −11.85 | 8.33 | −6.05 | −3.00 | 11.75 | 6.44 |
| Machinery and equipment | 18.84 | 5.48 | −0.94 | −8.00 | 7.17 | 10.36 |
| Transport equipment | 50.14 | 5.49 | 2.59 | −1.74 | −0.88 | 21.25 |
| Manufactures not elsewhere specified | 9.81 | 2.34 | 1.30 | −0.80 | 10.99 | −2.90 |
| Electricity | 0.07 | 0.43 | 0.43 | 0.90 | 0.95 | 1.16 |
| Construction | 16.02 | 2.71 | 2.27 | 6.01 | 3.17 | 2.06 |
| Trade services | 13.35 | 0.40 | 1.60 | 7.16 | 9.36 | −2.20 |
| Other transport | 8.37 | 1.79 | 3.55 | 3.16 | 6.12 | 10.13 |
| Water transport | 6.82 | 2.10 | 2.23 | 5.54 | 2.05 | 9.02 |
| Air transport | 7.78 | 5.83 | 4.12 | 8.80 | −0.57 | 5.81 |
| Hospitality services | −2.64 | −5.33 | −1.33 | 1.01 | 1.21 | −8.44 |
| Other business services | −1.25 | −4.22 | −0.04 | 0.18 | −0.93 | −12.68 |
| Other services | −0.20 | −1.69 | −0.18 | 0.00 | −0.78 | −3.01 |
| Agriculture | 8.55 | 0.64 | 3.08 | 2.38 | −2.96 | 2.59 |
| Manufacturing | 7.01 | 4.44 | 0.68 | 3.56 | 5.40 | 1.60 |
| Services | 3.97 | −0.91 | 1.43 | 2.53 | 0.25 | −2.21 |
| Other | −0.90 | −2.19 | 1.19 | −0.14 | 0.59 | −1.28 |
| Total | 1.89 | 3.75 | 0.95 | 1.45 | 3.67 | 1.18 |

*Source:* Maliszewska and van der Mensbrugghe 2019.

## 2.3 IMPACT ON INCOME, WELFARE, AND POVERTY

### *Trade effects on aggregate income and welfare*

The reduction in trade costs due to BRI projects would increase global real income due to increases in income for both Belt and Road corridor economies and non-Belt and Road corridor countries. In the CGE simulation, the reduction in trade costs due to the BRI leads to a global real income increase of 0.7 percent in 2030 relative to the baseline (figure 2.5), not including the cost of infrastructure investment (see chapter 1).[10] This is sizable compared with the estimates of other CGE models of the real income impact of global free trade of around 1 percent. The Belt and Road corridor economies capture 70 percent of this gain, with an increase in China's real income that is equal to 20 percent of the total global gain. Overall, the new infrastructure network would increase real incomes for corridor economies by 1.2 percent—and for non-Belt and Road economies by 0.3 percent.

Real income gains from BRI projects range between 1 percent for East Asia and Pacific and 2 percent for corridor economies in Sub-Saharan Africa. These positive income effects are driven by the reallocation of resources induced by the reduction in trade costs. With cheaper or higher quality inputs imported, resources are reallocated to increase productivity, improve exports, and boost incomes. Countries like Pakistan and the Kyrgyz Republic are expected to experience the largest gains in real income, respectively 10.5 and 10.4 percent higher than the baseline. The new BRI projects are expected to mostly improve these countries' access to their export markets. East Asian economies are expected to have sizable gains: Thailand (8.2 percent), Malaysia (7.7 percent), Cambodia (5.0 percent), and Lao PDR (3.1 percent). Other countries with large gains in real income are Bangladesh (6.9 percent), Turkey (3.6 percent), the Islamic Republic of Iran (3.0 percent), and Tanzania (2.5 percent).

The effects of BRI transport infrastructure projects on GDP tend to be larger in the structural model (see figure 2.5). BRI projects are expected to increase world GDP by 2.9 percent—the increase for non-Belt and Road economies at 2.6 percent and for corridor economies at 3.4 percent. While larger than the impact of the CGE model, these estimates in the structural model of the real income effect of BRI infrastructure are in line with estimates in the related literature. Using a similar model, Donaldson (2018) found that the vast network of railroads built in colonial India (Bangladesh, India, and Pakistan) toward the end of the 19th century and the beginning of the 20th century increased real income by 16 percent. As seen in the previous section, the larger gains from the structural models mostly accrue as the reduction in trade costs has a greater effect on trade, particularly in intermediate goods, leading to larger reallocations of resources and productivity gains.

---

[10] In the CGE model, welfare is measured as the equivalent variation for households, which is similar in magnitude to real private consumption.

Figure 2.5: Infrastructure improvements are projected to increase GDP (CGE and SGE models)

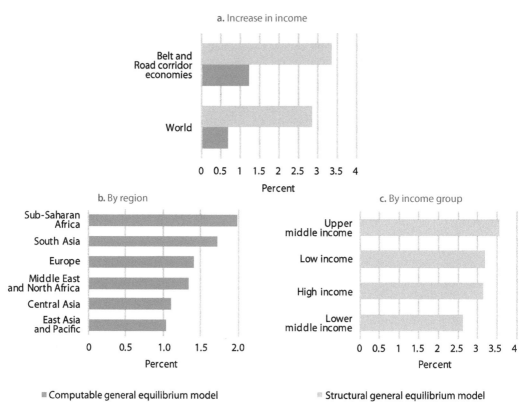

**a.** Increase in income

**b.** By region

**c.** By income group

■ Computable general equilibrium model    ■ Structural general equilibrium model

*Source:* Maliszewska and van der Mensbrugghe 2019; de Soyres, Mulabdic, and Ruta 2019.

Upper-middle- and low-income corridor economies are expected to benefit the most from the infrastructure improvement.

The result for upper-middle-income countries is driven by China's improved access to foreign markets, estimated to increase its GDP by 3.4 percent. The impact for low-income countries is driven by the corridor economies in Sub-Saharan Africa as the new ports in Tanzania and Kenya could substantially improve the connectivity of those two countries to other corridor economies and the rest of the world.

The welfare impact of BRI transport projects and the distribution of gains across countries need to account for the cost of building the infrastructure. The structural model compares the long-term real income gains for each country with an estimate of the share of the BRI infrastructure cost that each country is expected to pay.[11] Corridor economies as a group

---

[11] In the SGE model, welfare is defined as total consumer revenues divided by the relevant consumption price index. Total revenue takes into account payments to factors of production, revenues derived from the portfolio shares and from import tariffs, and the cost of the transport infrastructures.

enjoy a net welfare gain of 2.8 percent. Because trade gains are not commensurate with project investment, Azerbaijan, Mongolia, and Tajikistan have a net welfare loss due to the high cost of infrastructure (de Soyres, Mulabdic, and Ruta 2019). Because the final cost of large transport projects is often substantially larger than their expected costs (see chapter 1), welfare losses could be a risk for a larger spectrum of countries. This highlights the importance of complementary reforms that improve the integration gains from transport projects (chapter 3), efficiency in public procurement (chapter 4), and managing the fiscal risks of infrastructure projects (chapter 4). The impact for non–Belt and Road economies is higher as they benefit from reductions in trade costs without bearing any costs related to the new infrastructure.

## Trade effects on poverty

Through its impact on integration and growth, the Belt and Road Initiative could reduce the percentage of people living in extreme poverty, with less than PPP US$1.90 a day. Under baseline conditions, it is expected that global extreme poverty will fall from 9.5 percent in 2015 to 3.9 percent by 2030 (CGE model). At the global level, BRI-related investments could lift 7.6 million from extreme poverty (these effects abstract from the cost of infrastructure investment that could affect household income through changes in government spending and taxation). The benefits extend to 4.3 million in Belt and Road corridor economies and 3.3 million in non–Belt and Road countries.

BRI-related investments could additionally lift up to 32 million people from moderate poverty, with less than PPP US$3.20 a day, with 26.7 million from corridor economies and 5.3 million from non–Belt and Road countries. Such higher poverty lines are more adequate for measuring poverty as countries leave low-income status (Jolliffe and Prydz 2016; Ravallion and Chen 2011).[12] The global percentage of people below the moderate poverty line was estimated at 25.8 percent in 2015 and is projected to decline to 10.4 percent by 2030 under business-as-usual conditions.

In Kenya and Tanzania, an additional 700,000 poor people would be expected to be lifted from extreme poverty by 2030. This is approximately equivalent to an additional 1.0 and 0.9 percentage point reduction in the extreme poverty headcount. In South Asia, Pakistan would see additional reductions in extreme poverty for 1.1 million people; Bangladesh is expected to see 200,000 people lifted out of extreme poverty (0.11 percent of headcount) (table 2.3).

---

[12] The World Bank recently adopted a new series of poverty lines better aligned with country-specific poverty lines.

**Table 2.3:** Impact of the BRI on poverty
(Poverty headcount ratios, percent, PPP US$1.90 a day)

| | Bangladesh | | | Kenya | | |
|---|---|---|---|---|---|---|
| **Scenario** | **2015** | **2030** | **Change** | **2015** | **2030** | **Change** |
| Baseline | 15.16 | 0.24 | | 37.29 | 19.32 | |
| New infrastructure | 15.16 | 0.13 | 0.11 | 37.29 | 18.34 | 0.98 |
| | Pakistan | | | Tanzania | | |
| **Scenario** | **2015** | **2030** | **Change** | **2015** | **2030** | **Change** |
| Baseline | 5.33 | 0.63 | | 40.69 | 9.03 | |
| New infrastructure | 5.33 | 0.18 | 0.45 | 40.69 | 8.17 | 0.86 |

*Source:* Maliszewska and van der Mensbrugghe 2019.

## *Effects through foreign investment*

The BRI could bring additional gains in growth through FDI flows not captured in the CGE and structural model simulations. FDI flows to BRI transport projects could increase Belt and Road corridor economies' annual GDP growth by 0.09 percentage points on average (Chen and Lin 2018). Corridor economies in Sub-Saharan Africa are expected to gain around 0.23 percentage points in GDP growth from the 7.47 percent increase in FDI flows, while South Asia and Central Asia are expected grow by 0.14 and 0.12 percentage points faster as a result of FDI increases of 6.25 and 7.28 percent respectively (figure 2.6). The positive effects of FDI on GDP growth diminish with income. BRI projects can also stimulate growth through FDI in non-Belt and Road countries, including a 0.13 percentage-point increase in non-BRI Sub-Saharan countries' GDP growth, through spillovers from the improved transport network.

**Figure 2.6:** The BRI transport network will increase GDP growth through foreign direct investment
(Percentage point increase in annual GDP growth)

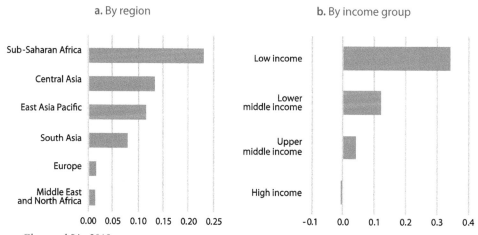

*Source:* Chen and Lin 2018.

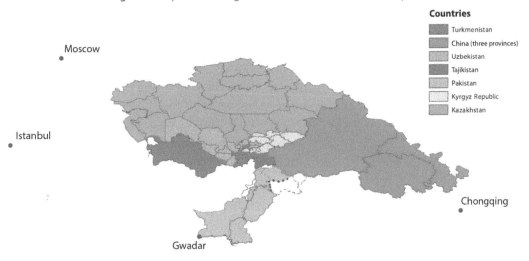

**Figure 2.7:** Spatial coverage of Central Asia used for the analysis

*Source:* Bird, Lebrand, and Venables 2019.

## Spatially differentiated effects of the BRI

Insights from new economic geography suggest that improvements in connectivity are likely to be associated with more spatial concentration, not dispersion of economic activity within countries, since firms tend to increase scale and benefit from agglomeration economies by locating near other firms engaged in similar and related activities. In the absence of mechanisms to compensate places that face "net economic losses" from connectivity improvements, policymakers are likely to see considerable risks in supporting initiatives that exacerbate spatial inequalities and pose fiscal burdens, while some subnational regions simply see trucks and rail wagons pass by while having to service the debt associated with infrastructure investments.

Spatial analysis is data-intensive and, hence, it is difficult to apply it to the 71 Belt and Road corridor economies. In this study, we focus on Central Asia, where BRI investments have the potential to spatially reorient the economic geography, due to the region's proximity to China and limited regional integration, and its Soviet legacy for current economic structures and trade links.[13] Central Asia is defined broadly to include three provinces in Western China, Kazakhstan, the Kyrgyz Republic, Pakistan, Tajikistan, Turkmenistan, and Uzbekistan (figure 2.7). Driving the potential gains from BRI investments are the improved opportunities for local producers and workers to access markets and suppliers. Shaping subnational region adjustments are the magnitude of improved market

---

[13] The analysis combines insights from research in new economic geography, a policy framework developed in the World Bank's World Development Report Reshaping Economic Geography (World Bank 2009) and lessons from two recent papers. The first (Bird, Lebrand, and Venables 2019) considers shifts in economic geography across many countries together, all of which are divided into subnational units (cities or regions). The second (Lall and Lebrand 2019) examines economic geography in each country, where internal geography responds to external integration and domestic transport investments.

access, the local comparative advantage (primary factor endowments, technology, and preferences), the mobility of people, and the changes in technology that allow for scale and clustering.

In the absence of institutional measures that enhance trade linkages, investments in transport infrastructure by themselves have modest impacts on reshaping the spatial economy (table 2.4). Kazakhstan benefits the most, closely followed by the Kyrgyz Republic, Tajikistan, and Pakistan, in that order. Turkmenistan reaps the smallest direct benefit; initial low levels of trade between Turkmenistan and other countries mean that the direct reductions in transport costs do not map into large impacts on trade costs. In aggregate, with no economic adjustment, the BRI infrastructure leads to a 1.4 percent real income gain for the region.

Real income growth is more than three times the size of the direct effect for the Kyrgyz Republic, while it is smaller than the direct effect for Turkmenistan and particularly Kazakhstan. At the aggregate level, monopolistic competition increases the real income gain to 1.9 percent, which is 36 percent greater than the direct effect. At the national level, there is a slight narrowing in dispersion of the gains across countries. The Kyrgyz Republic has a smaller, though still large, benefit over the Armington case, whereas the western China provinces, Kazakhstan, and Pakistan, all with a large manufacturing base, now observe a greater positive benefit from the BRI. Aggregate gains are substantially larger, with a total impact on

**Table 2.4:** Real income gains by economy
(Percent)

| | Direct effect of transport cost decline | Average real income growth | | |
|---|---|---|---|---|
| | | Armington benchmark | Monopolistic competition | Increasing returns and labor mobility |
| China (three provinces) | 1.2 | 1.2 | 2.0 | 2.5 |
| Kazakhstan | 1.9 | 1.6 | 2.1 | 5.2 |
| Kyrgyz Republic | 1.6 | 4.9 | 4.4 | 4.6 |
| Pakistan | 1.5 | 1.8 | 2.3 | 6.3 |
| Tajikistan | 1.6 | 1.7 | 1.5 | 1.0 |
| Turkmenistan | 0.4 | 0.3 | 0.0 | −0.3 |
| Uzbekistan | 0.7 | 0.8 | 1.0 | 1.6 |
| Aggregate | 1.4 | 1.4 | 1.9 | 4.0 |

*Source:* Bird, Lebrand, and Venables 2019.
*Note:* The first column shows the direct impact of the transport cost decline on trade costs (the change in the base—trade-weighted index of transport costs). This assumes that there is no response whatsoever to trade or output in any district or country: it can be thought of as simply measuring the extent to which each place is directly affected. The subsequent columns give effects under different assumptions about the type of economic response. The second column (Armington) is based on the assumption by Paul Armington in 1969—that products traded internationally are differentiated by country of origin. This is the standard assumption of international CGE models. The third column, monopolistic competition, allows manufacturing firms to relocate in response to changes in their profitability. The final column models both increasing returns to scale in manufacturing production and labor mobility between districts within each country in response to changing within-country wage differences.

the region of 4 percent, nearly three times the direct effect. The countries receiving the most additional benefit from this include the three China provinces, Kazakhstan, Uzbekistan, and particularly Pakistan, whose growth in real income is more than four times the direct effect. Tajikistan and Turkmenistan experience lower income growth than under the previous assumption, with growth even turning negative for Turkmenistan.

Some districts reap large benefits from the fall in transport costs, far above the direct effects, while other districts see a fall in real income (figure 2.8). This creates some higher spatial inequalities within and across countries. The spatial differential is further accentuated in the presence of increasing returns, which allow for clustering.

**Figure 2.8:** Spatial disaggregation of real income growth against direct effects of transport investments at district level

a. Spatially differentiated impacts on growth in real incomes (Armington)

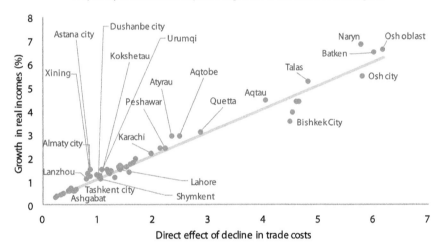

b. Spatially differentiated impacts on growth in real incomes (increasing returns and labor mobility)

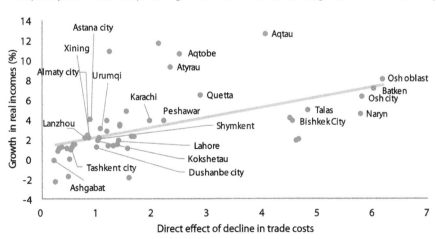

*Source:* Bird, Lebrand, and Venables 2019.

So how do real income effects add up to around four times larger than the direct effect of changing transport times? The degree to which countries and districts can benefit from these economies of scale depends on three major factors. First, with fluid labor mobility, population movements are large, allowing some districts to increase population; achieving these gains requires growing areas to accommodate this extra population. Second, the districts' comparative advantage in manufacturing affects their income growth. Countries with districts where manufacturing productivity is high are in a position to allow these districts to grow and generate clusters. Third, in industries where specialization and clustering are possible, regional trade costs become more important for growth. These effects are likely to be driving potential gains in western Kazakhstan, the Kyrgyz Republic, and Pakistan. For example, there is potential for major income gains in Pakistan, around the metropolitan area of Karachi, as well as smaller cities such as Quetta, and Peshawar, with magnitudes four times the direct gains from trade cost declines. These locations are the most likely to benefit from urban clustering and increasing returns in manufacturing-led tradables.

# CHAPTER 3

## Complementary policies and institutions

Despite the importance of infrastructure to development, only in conjunction with complementary policies and institutions will countries maximize the benefits from BRI transport projects. Policies that promote integration, inclusiveness, connectivity, and private sector development, will be critical force multipliers for project investments.

In some instances, Belt and Road corridor economies can take domestic actions to support infrastructure development. Corridor planning and management that fully account for the costs and benefits of projects, directly and indirectly, will reduce the risks of stranded infrastructure. Reducing trade facilitation hurdles will lower trading costs and increase integration, independent of infrastructure investments. Likewise, making the business environment more favorable for private participation in infrastructure financing can reduce fiscal risks and ensure the long-term sustainability of projects. In other instances, greater cross-border cooperation will be needed to allow BRI investments to produce their full effects. Countries can reduce tariffs and non-tariff barriers through international trade agreements and promote foreign direct investment (FDI) through coordinated reforms of their investment regimes and dispute settlement mechanisms.

## 3.1 PROMOTING INTEGRATION

Trade reforms could magnify the gains from the new and improved infrastructure network. This chapter analyzes the impact on exports and real income of two scenarios of complementary trade policy reform: trade facilitation reform (a 50 percent reduction in border delays for Belt and Road corridor economies), and tariff reform (a 50 percent cut in bilateral tariffs among corridor economies). While such a large-scale, coordinated trade policy reform may be difficult in practice, the scenarios stress the importance of complementary reforms for the BRI to substantially improve trade integration. Results from the various models show that the aggregate effects of combining the infrastructure improvements with reforms would be between 2 and 4 times higher than when infrastructure projects are not combined with policy reform. The section also considers the effects of two other types of reform that affect policies both at the border and behind the border (such as domestic regulation): the deepening of trade agreements, and the liberalization of service trade.

### *Trade and real income impact of lowering border delays*

Policies to promote trade facilitation in Belt and Road corridor economies would boost their exports, thus complementing infrastructure projects. In the computable general equilibrium (CGE) analysis, a reduction in border delays would magnify the effects of BRI transport projects on exports from corridor economies by more than 1.5 percentage points (figure 3.1a). If in addition to an improved infrastructure network, border delays were reduced by half, corridor economies could experience export

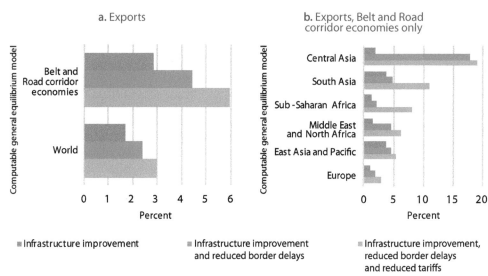

**Figure 3.1:** Impact of complementary policies on exports (CGE)

**a.** Exports

**b.** Exports, Belt and Road corridor economies only

- ■ Infrastructure improvement
- ■ Infrastructure improvement and reduced border delays
- ■ Infrastructure improvement, reduced border delays and reduced tariffs

*Source:* Maliszewska and van der Mensbrugghe 2019.

growth of 4.4 percent. This effect is not surprising given the long delays at the border in many corridor economies (chapter 1). Reducing these frictions allows firms to import a larger variety of inputs essential in production in a timely manner, thus increasing efficiency and exports. The structural model finds that reducing border delays would magnify the impact of infrastructure projects on BRI exports by a factor of 3.

Complementing BRI transport infrastructure projects with reductions in border delays is a priority for Central Asia and for low-income corridor economies. Reducing border delays can increase exports of Central Asian economies by 18 percent (figure 3.1b). While large, this result is not surprising given the major border delays documented for Central Asia. All other corridor economies have export gains that range between 1.8 percent for Eastern Europe and 4.8 percent for South Asia, pointing to the importance of reducing border delays for most corridor economies. Implementing border management reforms would magnify the trade effect of BRI projects, but their implementation is complex (box 3.1).

Complementing BRI projects with border delay reductions would increase real incomes for corridor economies and non-Belt and Road countries. As a result of reduced border delays combined with BRI transport infrastructure projects, the real income of corridor economies would increase by 2 percent, while global real income and the real income of non-Belt and Road economies would increase by 1 and 0.4 percent respectively (figure 3.2a). Consistent with the findings on trade, real income gains would be particularly large for Central Asia (11.3 percent) and positive for all

**Box 3.1:** Reducing trade facilitation hurdles along BRI corridors

Based on the analysis in Bartley Johns et al. (2018), this box focuses on five common themes that should be priorities to improve trade facilitation along BRI corridors.

- Greater coordination among agencies, particularly along corridors, is needed to implement key trade facilitation reforms. National trade facilitation committees should play a central role, and they should take on BRI-related trade facilitation reforms, in the context of other efforts such as implementing the Trade Facilitation Agreement of the World Trade Organization (WTO-TFA).

- Regulatory transparency needs to improve. Trade information portals have been implemented in a number of Belt and Road corridor economies, and their use is expected to grow as members come into compliance with their WTO obligations. As well as being beneficial in itself, reform to improve transparency is a stepping stone to other, more ambitious trade facilitation reform, including implementing national and regional single window systems.

- Risk-based approaches to border management are needed, especially in agencies other than customs. Information on trade transactions needs to be shared by governments along specific corridors, in order to facilitate legitimate shipments. Information sharing can also support risk profiling so that resources are directed more effectively.

- Substantial additional trade transaction costs and procedural inefficiencies are generated by non-customs agencies. Greater information sharing by agencies involved in standards-related approvals is needed, both within and among governments. Beyond information sharing, mutual recognition of conformity assessments would have a greater impact and pave the way for eventual mutual recognition of standards.

- Effective transit regimes need to be implemented for each BRI corridor.

Identifying the challenges facing corridor economies in facilitating trade along the key corridors is a necessary first step—but early attention needs to be given to how reforms will be designed and implemented most effectively. Bartley Johns et al. (2018) make four recommendations:

- Undertake corridor-by-corridor diagnostics of trade facilitation constraints, given the limited evidence base. These should focus on the five themes identified above, as well as any other relevant issues identified for each corridor.

- Develop reform action plans for each corridor, based on improving trade facilitation outcomes. These action plans would identify the most effective sequencing of reforms, and include monitoring frameworks to track progress in reform implementation. The action plans would need to reflect an appropriate balance of reforms to be implemented regionally, while recognizing that countries will need to manage most of the burden for implementation.

- Develop appropriate coordination mechanisms and associated institutions to support active collaboration among corridor economies to exchange data, operational information, and best practices; build regulatory consistency; and address trade facilitation–related problems.

- Draw on international standards and accepted good practice principles for trade facilitation wherever possible.

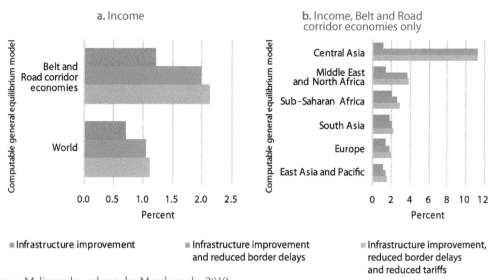

**Figure 3.2:** Impact of complementary policies on income (CGE)

a. Income

b. Income, Belt and Road corridor economies only

Infrastructure improvement

Infrastructure improvement and reduced border delays

Infrastructure improvement, reduced border delays and reduced tariffs

*Source:* Maliszewska and van der Mensbrugghe 2019.

other regions (figure 3.2b). The structural model suggests that if the BRI reduced border delays by 50 percent, the GDP of corridor economies would expand by 6.4 percent, thanks to the higher efficiency gains associated with the expansion of international trade. The largest GDP gains would be concentrated in low-income economies.

Complementary trade facilitation reforms would reduce poverty in corridor economies and beyond. With the reduction in border delays, global poverty would be further reduced by the additional 6.5 million for the extreme poverty line and 12.6 million for the moderate poverty line. Overall in the Belt and Road corridor economies, more than 3.7 million would be lifted from extreme poverty by reduced border delays, or 0.7 percent of the total population, by 2030. More than 7.6 million would be lifted from moderate poverty under the same assumptions.

### *Spatial impact of lowering border delays*

The spatial impacts of BRI transport infrastructure reported in chapter 2 would be diminished without complementary reforms in trade policy and border improvements. These reforms imply larger aggregate gains from the reallocation of economic activity between different districts, but also more dispersion of the effects. This section illustrates this point analyzing the expected spatial impacts in Central Asia of combining infrastructure upgrades with reduced border costs.

Reducing border costs alongside infrastructure improvements increases the share of the reduction in trade costs coming from within the region. Kazakhstan has a 1.1 percent reduction in regional trade costs but 0.3 percent with infrastructure improvements

**Table 3.1:** Impacts of declining transport costs on real incomes
(Percent)

| Countries | Infrastructure | | Border time | | Borders and infrastructure | |
|---|---|---|---|---|---|---|
| | Armington benchmark | Increasing returns and labor mobility | Armington benchmark | Increasing returns and labor mobility | Armington benchmark | Increasing returns and labor mobility |
| China (three provinces) | 1.2 | 2.5 | 3.3 | 7.4 | 5.5 | 13.1 |
| Kazakhstan | 1.6 | 5.2 | 3.0 | 0.2 | 4.8 | 6.0 |
| Kyrgyz Republic | 4.9 | 4.6 | 6.9 | 8.1 | 12.8 | 16.0 |
| Pakistan | 1.8 | 6.3 | 3.4 | 8.9 | 5.5 | 12.8 |
| Tajikistan | 1.7 | 1.0 | 3.8 | 1.4 | 6.2 | 1.9 |
| Turkmenistan | 0.3 | −0.3 | 1.9 | −4.1 | 2.2 | −4.5 |
| Uzbekistan | 0.8 | 1.6 | 2.5 | 6.2 | 3.6 | 7.0 |
| Aggregate | 1.4 | 4.0 | 3.1 | 5.8 | 5.0 | 9.9 |

*Source:* Bird, Lebrand, and Venables 2019.
*Note:* Manufacturing firms relocate in response to changes in their profitability.

only. Under the conservative benchmark case (Armington), aggregate gains of 5 percent are substantially larger than the 1.4 percent estimated for infrastructure alone (table 3.1). Real income growth is more than that of infrastructure alone for each country, and more than seven times higher for Turkmenistan, and at least three times higher for Kazakhstan, the Kyrgyz Republic, Pakistan, Tajikistan, and Uzbekistan. Aggregate gains are substantially larger for the models with increasing returns to scale in manufacturing production and labor mobility between districts within each country in response to intra–country wage differences, with a total impact on the region of 9.9 percent. The countries that receive the most additional benefit from this include the three China districts, Pakistan, and Uzbekistan. Tajikistan and Turkmenistan experience lower income growth than under the previous assumption, with the negative growth sharper in Turkmenistan.

The provision of complementary border reforms amplifies the spatial response to the BRI (figure 3.3). As with infrastructure alone, some districts reap large benefits from the fall in transport costs, far above the direct effects, while other districts see a fall in real income. However, reduced border delays tend to magnify impacts for each place, with a steeper drop in income for Ashgabat, while most districts see greater income gains, and a greater number of cities enjoy gains above 10 percent.

### Tariffs and trade agreements

Reducing tariffs among Belt and Road corridor economies would create more trade among participating economies, but also some trade diversion with non-Belt and Road economies. Unlike reductions in border delays, which tend to reduce trade costs for all countries, tariffs can be reduced in a discriminatory (preferential) manner for different countries. The result is that

**Figure 3.3:** Change in real incomes at the district level from reducing border costs and investing in transport infrastructure
(Percent)

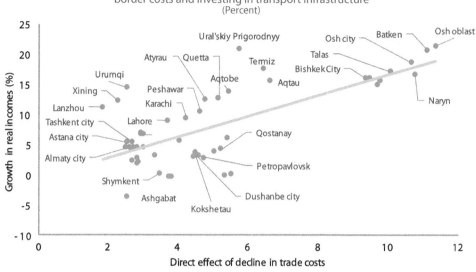

*Source:* Bird, Lebrand, and Venables 2019.
*Note:* The figure reproduces the district level scatter plot of real income responses to infrastructure improvements to include declines in trade costs of border reforms combined with infrastructure, thus allowing for increasing returns to scale and factor mobility.

this policy reform has positive effects on within-BRI trade and ambiguous effects on non–Belt and Road economies. To quantify these effects, the analysis simulates a 50-percent reduction in applied tariffs among corridor economies. A combination of BRI infrastructure projects, reduced border delays, and preferential tariff cuts would boost exports of corridor economies by 5.9 percent (see figure 3.1a). World trade would still increase by 2.9 percent, but non–Belt and Road economies would see their exports grow by only 0.3 percent. In the structural model, trade effects are larger than with the computable model. In addition, despite the preferential nature of the tariff reform, the impact on non–Belt and Road economies' exports is still positive, driven by the more important complementarities in production assumed in the structural model.

Exports of all corridor economies would grow as infrastructure projects are complemented by tariff reforms, but there are significant differences by region. Average tariffs in corridor economies are higher than those in advanced economies, but they vary from around 14 percent in Sub-Saharan Africa and South Asia to 2 percent in East Asia and Pacific. Tariff reductions would boost the effect of BRI projects by 6 percentage points for the two most protected regions, with exports expanding by 11 percent for South Asia and 8.2 percent for Sub-Saharan Africa (see figure 3.1b). Other regions also experience higher exports, but to less extent. For economies in Eastern Europe and East Asia and Pacific, the benefit of trade policy in addition to infrastructure investment and trade facilitation is relatively small.

Preferential tariff reductions have the potential to further increase real income of corridor economies and the world but have an ambiguous effect on non–Belt and Road economies. The combined effect of these reforms is to increase real income of the economies on the

Belt and Road by 2.1 percent and global income by 1.1 percent (figure 3.3a). The real income of the non–Belt and Road corridor economies is slightly lower relative to the scenario with border delay reductions as the discriminatory tariff cuts divert exports from this area. The preferential reduction of tariffs within Belt and Road economies brings only marginal poverty reductions. An additional 0.34 million would be lifted from extreme poverty and 1.7 from moderate poverty by 2030, compared with the scenario with infrastructure improvements and border delay reductions, mostly along the Belt and Road corridors. The structural model finds that the impact of combined policy reforms (reduced border delays and tariffs) would increase Belt and Road corridor economies' GDP by a factor of 4 relative to the scenario where only infrastructure is improved. The combined policy reforms increase global GDP by a factor of 3. Consistent with the CGE model, most of the gains for non–Belt and Road economies come from the reduction in trade costs due to transport infrastructure and border delays.

Deeper forms of trade agreement may be politically more difficult, but they would provide a further boost to BRI trade. Analysis based on a gravity model shows that trade agreements that go beyond tariffs ("deep" trade agreements) and include policy areas such as services, investment, and competition policy, could further contribute to trade integration. If corridor economies signed a trade agreement as deep as the regional average, intraregional trade would increase by 16 percent (Baniya, Rocha, and Ruta 2018). Intuitively, deepening trade agreements would allow corridor economies to reduce trade costs below the barriers created by border restrictions such as tariffs and cumbersome border procedures. It would also alleviate the fragmentation of rules across corridor economies that constrains regional and global value chains (box 3.2).

## 3.2 POLICIES AND INSTITUTIONS TO PROMOTE CORRIDOR DEVELOPMENT

A corridor has three main intertwined dimensions: infrastructure, services, and the institutions that coordinate corridor activities. Infrastructure needs to be planned, procured, built, operated, and maintained to provide the transportation services users demand. Infrastructure needs to be funded and financed. In transnational corridors, policies, procedures, standards, and regulations need to be harmonized for seamless provision of transport services. Effective implementation of all these activities requires coordination, particularly in transnational corridors.

### *Project development*

#### Planning

Project selection is one of the most important challenges for the BRI. The most important step in corridor planning is selecting the location and type of corridor infrastructure that will be built. The long economic life of transport infrastructure creates path dependency and sets a corridor, and the countries it traverses, on an irreversible path. Avoiding stranded infrastructure requires robust and sound planning that selects corridor infrastructure with the highest net benefits considering potential risks. Transport corridors should be part of national and regional plans to maximize their benefits, as in Kazakhstan, where the government prepared an infrastructure development plan (Linn and Zucker 2019).

**Box 3.2:** Services trade reform

A well-functioning services sector is essential for the full realization of the BRI's expected benefits. Improved access to finance, communications, transport, and other services, either through unilateral reforms or trade agreements, enhances firm productivity and other aspects of the performance of firms (Constantinescu, Mattoo, and Ruta 2018). Added urgency for service reform stems from the fact that goods trade and services trade are increasingly intertwined, as value added produced in a wide range of services is increasingly embodied in manufactured goods traded internationally.[1]

Belt and Road corridor economies' services trade is generally more restricted than in G7 countries, but there is variation by region. These conclusions emerge from an examination of the World Bank's Services Trade Restrictiveness Index (STRI), a measure that provides a snapshot of the level of services trade protectionism as of 2012 and is available for 49 of the 71 corridor economies. Indeed, for corridor economies in all regions except Europe and Central Asia, the STRI is on average higher than the average STRI in G7 countries. The most restrictive regions are the Middle East and North Africa and South Asia (figure B3.2.1).

**Figure B3.2.1:** Overall Services Trade Restrictiveness Index of Belt and Road corridor economies

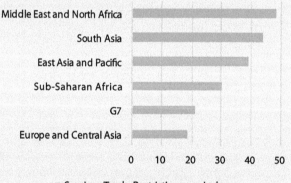

■ Services Trade Restrictiveness Index

*Source:* World Bank Services Trade Restrictions Database.

Moreover, regional patterns of services trade restrictiveness differ from those of goods trade restrictiveness.

• First, corridor economies in the Middle East and North Africa are the most restrictive for services trade, and those in Sub-Saharan Africa and South Asia for goods trade. Within the Middle East and North Africa, the Arab Republic of Egypt, the Islamic Republic of Iran, Kuwait, and Qatar each have STRIs of about 50 percent; the least restrictive country in the group is Yemen, with an STRI of 32 percent.

---

[1] See Hallward-Driemeier and Nayyar 2018 for a discussion of the trends and the implications of deepening interlinkages between manufacturing and services sectors, as in the "servicification" of manufacturing.

• Second, different from goods trade, the average STRI of corridor economies in Europe and Central Asia is below the ones for both G7 and other regions. Except for Belarus, all 17 countries reporting have STRIs of less than 30 percent. In addition, four of the 17 countries—Armenia, Georgia, Lithuania, and Poland—have STRIs below 14.3, the level of the United Kingdom, the least restrictive country in the G7. Central Asian countries such as Kazakhstan (15.2 percent) and the Kyrgyz Republic (17 percent) also have low STRIs.

• Even with their relatively low tariffs, corridor economies in East Asia and Pacific are more restrictive in services trade than corridor economies in both Europe and Central Asia and Sub-Saharan Africa. Of eight corridor economies with data in East Asia and Pacific, six have STRIs above 30 percent. The most restrictive country is the Philippines, with an STRI of 53.5 percent.

STRIs at the sectoral level shed more light on the regional patterns at the aggregate level (figure B3.2.2). First, corridor economies in the Middle East and North Africa are the most restrictive in all sectors of focus, except transport services. Second, the openness of services for corridor economies in Europe and Central Asia relative to the G7 is driven by retail and professional services. Third, corridor economies in East Asia and Pacific have significant barriers to trade in all five sectors, especially in professional services. Transport services are most restrictive in South Asia.

**Figure B3.2.2:** Services Trade Restrictions Index of Belt and Road corridor economies by sector

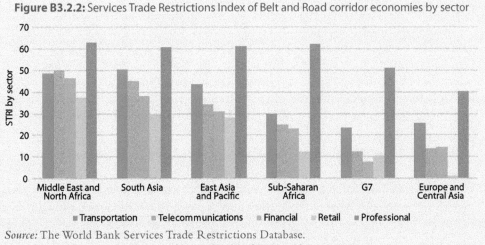

*Source:* The World Bank Services Trade Restrictions Database.
*Note:* The STRI provides data as of 2012, for 49 of 71 corridor economies.

A robust project appraisal must be based on clear analysis that sets out possible mechanisms for wider impacts. Conventional transport cost-benefit appraisal typically focuses on the user benefits of a transport improvement and does not consider wider economic impacts. Appraisal should avoid double counting both between wider impacts and user benefits and between different wider impacts (Laird and Venables 2017). Otherwise, investments that do not make sense could end up being legitimized. For instance, the role of subsidies and of individual corridors in the entire transport network need to be explicitly accounted for in the evaluation, especially since different corridors compete for the same traffic (box 3.3). Different methodologies quantify different impacts of transport infrastructure, so sound appraisal should use the methodology best suited to capture the mechanisms set out in the theory of change of each specific project (ADB et al. 2018; Laird and Venables 2017).

Improving the valuation of BRI investments should consider the following aspects (Duranton and Venables 2018):

- *Quantity change.* There should be a full description of the expected quantity changes arising from the project, including further economic activity likely to be created by the investment. The description should separate clearly the direct and indirect effects—distinguishing between

---

**Box 3.3:** The impact of removing subsidies for rail freight

Many China–Europe rail freight services are subsidized by local governments. Inland cities such as Chengdu originally did this to provide an attractive transport option to Europe that would draw foreign manufacturers from their historic sites near the coast. Cities closer to the coast, such as Yiwu, then followed to ensure that they could compete with the inland cities. The central government's emphasis on the BRI, and the targets given to various provinces, led to further discounting to meet annual targets of freight dispatched.

Cities began to attract freight from other areas by providing heavily discounted (or free) feeder services. For example, in Chengdu, the subsidy peaked in 2017 at more than 65 percent of the actual cost to reach the target of 1,000 block trains. More than 60 percent of the freight came from or went to shippers outside the Chengdu region in 2017. In Chongqing, the rate for a 40-foot carrier-owned container for freight originating from outside its region is US$1,000 cheaper than that from Southwest China—to attract more traffic.

The subsidies could thus be seen either as a short-term reaction to targets or as a necessary step in promoting traffic so that service frequency can be reasonable, which will generate traffic in its own right. But the China–Central Asia freight rates have little or no subsidy, creating a distortion in favor of China–Europe freight. The Chengdu–Hamburg rate is US$2,150 while Chengdu–Astana is about US$3,000 on a combined rate—or US$2,700 on a through rate if one exists.

What would happen if subsidies ceased—would the market revert to what it was five or six years ago? Or would traffic decline merely temporarily before resuming its growth, albeit at a lower rate than in the past three years? Subsidies range from under 50 percent to about 75 percent of the unsubsidized cost. Doubling the current rates, which in some cases would amount to less than a 100 percent removal of subsidies, would reduce the tonnage transported by rail between China and Europe to about half the current volume (Bullock, Liu, and Tan 2019)

the goods and services delivered and used by the project—and the quantity changes due to induced changes in private sector behavior. It should be accompanied by a description of the mechanisms for these quantity changes to arise, taking into account the possible displacement effects—the policy-induced relocation of economic activity between places.

• *Valuation of changes.* There should be analysis of why the project's quantity changes are of net social value, distinguishing between the value of direct and indirect effects. The latter may be of net social value because of the interaction of quantity changes with market failures and inefficient resource allocation; the magnitude of and reasons for any such market failures should be carefully diagnosed and evaluated. Net social value may also derive from equity concerns, which should be explicit.

• *Transparency.* The mechanisms underpinning both the quantity changes and their social value should be clear and explained in a manner that enables the key magnitudes to be understood from straightforward back-of-the-envelope calculation.

• *Sensitivity.* An analysis should describe the dependence of the quantity effects and their valuation on key assumptions about the economic environment. The quantitative importance of failures of these assumptions should be outlined.

• *Alternatives.* Any project should make a strong case that it provides the most cost-effective way to solve the main problem described in the theory of change.

## Funding and financing

Transport corridors can produce large socioeconomic benefits, but they also carry large costs. Depending on the beneficiaries' income, the operators' ability to control access, and the quality of services, some costs can be recovered from user charges. But a large share of the cost of corridors will be covered by general tax revenues (ADB et al. 2018), even if governments can monetize some of the wider economic benefits—such as increased trade, land use changes, and jobs—through taxes. Tax and user charge revenues accrue over time, while project costs are paid at the preparation, development, and construction stages. Large projects face a mismatch in the maturity of funding, which can be addressed by financing from the domestic or international financial system.[1]

It is much more difficult to secure funding for cross-border investments than for purely national projects. When benefits and costs are not proportionately shared, an uneven willingness to cover costs will arise. For example, when most of the traffic along a corridor is transit trade, countries only benefit from the corridor through the transit rates they might charge. This reduces the willingness of transit countries to fund corridor investments and maintenance, affecting the overall efficiency of the network.

---

[1] Funding and financing tend to be considered synonyms, but they are not. Who funds a project means who ultimately pays for it over the long term—that is, users and taxpayers. Who finances a project means who raises the cash to build it at the beginning. For example, a project can be financed by commercial debt, which taxpayers will have to repay over time.

## Harmonization and standardization

Interoperability is imperative for efficient and effective trade and transport flows. International corridors are in part intended to reduce fragmentation of jurisdictional, infrastructural, procedural, managerial, and other boundaries. Interoperability can be achieved by harmonizing laws, norms, standards, practices, and institutional frameworks based on internationally agreed standards. Agreements on standards—for example, for railway infrastructure and rolling stock, especially along the major international corridors—will enable vehicles and trains to travel across borders without costly transloading. Combining investments in transport and information and communications technology (ICT) would also improve corridor management (box 3.4). Other complementary policy reforms are discussed in the example of corridor development in Vietnam (box 3.5).

---

**Box 3.4:** Transport and information and communications technology synergies

The potential synergies between transport and ICT are accentuated under the BRI. On the infrastructure side, the "dig once" principle is most relevant. It collocates fiber optic cable alongside new roads, railways, and electric grids, substantially lowering overall investment costs. In the United States, estimates of cost savings range from 25 to 33 percent, particularly in densely populated areas where the complexity and cost of construction is highest, and about 15 percent in rural areas. Collocating fiber optic should be coordinated with all stakeholders to avoid unnecessary installations.

Big data and blockchain have the potential for transforming the transport and logistics industries and the way corridors are managed and used. Traditional corridor management and performance monitoring approaches rely on gathering data through trip diaries, stakeholders surveys, or detailed diagnostics of one or more specific components of the corridor. The traditional approaches, though useful, often provide only partial pictures in geographic and temporal space.

Big data analytics offer new capabilities for operational capacity assessments, strategic planning, and environmental monitoring. Different units along a corridor—such as cranes in ports, highways, trains, vehicles, vessels, individual shipments, containers, and phones carried by crews—increasingly have sensors that continuously stream data. The most common sensors provide information on the location of shipments (from GPS or wayside technologies), speed of movement, duration of stops, interruptions during movement, and temperature. When combined with other systems such as port, customs, and border stations, the various data can be highly informative about corridor performance.

Consortium blockchain networks along the BRI corridors—among producers, shippers, port operators, customs agencies, and buyers—could provide reliable proof of origin and trustworthy records of transportation routes and conditions, such as temperature and humidity during the transport of perishable goods. Having such trusted information available to all relevant participants could reduce the need for human inspection and paperwork at borders and provide assurance of the quality and compliance of the goods traded.

Improving corridor management would bring down shipping times by 7 percent along the China–Mongolia–Russia Economic Corridor and by up to 20 percent along the China–Pakistan Economic Corridor (de Soyres et al. 2018). The associated change in trade costs would range from 5 percent for the China–Mongolia–Russia Economic Corridor to 17 percent for the China–Pakistan Economic Corridor. All other corridors would fall between these two extremes. The benefits of improved corridor management are smaller for countries farther away from the corridors, as shipments use less efficient segments of the transport network to reach their final destinations (de Soyres et al. 2018).

---

**Box 3.5:** Successful corridor development—Vietnam National Highway N°. 5

The success of transport corridors are predicated by two factors: a substantial improvement in market access, and complementary national and subnational economic development policies.

Vietnam developed NH-5 in the 1990s as a 106-kilometer road connecting Hanoi and the Hai Phong port (ADB et al. 2018). Upgrades to the road, financed by Japanese aid, cut the transport time from Hanoi to Hai Phong from five hours to two and doubled the average vehicle speed from 24–30 kilometers per hour to 50–60 kilometers per hour.[1]

The NH-5 connected four existing industrial parks, one in Hanoi and three in Hai Phong, and since the road upgrades, eight new parks have been developed. Industrial clusters have also developed along the NH-5 for garments, food processing, machinery, and electronics. The industrial parks centered on "anchor tenants" including such global brands as Canon, Honda, and Panasonic. Anchor tenants were encouraged through incentives including tax reductions and holidays to invite affiliate companies and link to local vendors and suppliers (JICA 2008).

Alongside this transport development, the government invested in human capital and reformed the business environment, including increasing openness to trade. These reforms also attracted foreign direct investment to create hot spots around the highway for local businesses to use in building their supply chains and supported the legal status of local private companies, enabling them to collaborate more easily with foreign partners. The reforms spurred big increases in FDI in economic development across the NH-5 corridor. Feeder roads and upgrades to public transport supported local farmers.

From 2000 to 2004, after project completion, the number of enterprises in Hanoi grew by 221 percent and in Hai Phong by 141 percent. The main reason firms located in these areas was good connectivity over NH-5 (JICA 2009).

---

[1] See Hallward-Driemeier and Nayyar 2018 for a discussion of the trends and the implications of deepening interlinkages between manufacturing and services sectors, as in the "servicification" of manufacturing.

## Institutional arrangements

The transnational scope of BRI corridors makes the coordination role of institutions particularly important. Institutions play the role of defining the objectives of cooperation and collaboration, and the actions that each party will need to perform. The BRI relies in part on existing institutional mechanisms, but mainly on bilateral interstate agreements and project financing agreements that China has concluded with many partners (Kunaka 2018). Many of the bilateral agreements are in general terms, more to register political commitments than to reflect concrete measures.

Institutional roles and arrangements differ for BRI land corridors at different stages of development-ranging from the Bangladesh–China–India–Myanmar Corridor, which is largely at conceptual stage, to the Eurasian Land Bridge, which has several commercial services already operating (table 3.2).

Shaping the Belt and Road as a truly multilateral initiative would require moving beyond the bilateral arrangements. For monitoring and enforcement, the current bilateral relationships that China has cultivated and established may be appropriate in the short term, especially during the development phases of some corridors, but not appropriate during the operational phases, especially when mitigating the risks discussed in chapter 4. Long-term institutional governance arrangements could serve several roles, including institutionalizing coordination mechanisms, providing a platform for public information and transparency, and improving standards.

## 3.3 PROMOTING PRIVATE SECTOR PARTICIPATION

The BRI has thus far been driven predominantly by China's state-owned banks and state-owned enterprises (SOEs), with limited private participation (Cader et al. 2019). Central SOEs

Table 3.2: Institutional functions and arrangements for BRI corridors

| | Interstate agreements to develop specific segments of a network | Policy reforms to meet agreed objectives (economic, social, or political) | Financial closure for specific elements of a network | Targeted solutions for specific market segments |
|---|---|---|---|---|
| **Formal rules** | Example: China–Central Asia–West Asia | Example: China–Mongolia–Russia | Example: Eurasian Pakistan Economic Corridor | Example: Eurasian Land Bridge |
| **Rules and norms** | High-level commitment to jointly develop an interconnected network | Definition of common policy objectives | Screening and prioritization of projects | Market tests and road shows |
| | | Example: China–Indochina | | |
| **Norms** | Conceptual definition of a network | Definition of principles of cooperation | Determination of financing mechanisms | Identification of potential markets |
| | Example: Bangladesh–China–India–Myanmar Corridor | | | |

*Source:* Kunaka 2018.

have been involved in 3,116 BRI projects.[2] They account for 50 percent of infrastructure projects already under construction or planned, and 70 percent of the contract value of those projects.[3] State-owned banks, policy or commercially oriented, represent most BRI-related project financing so far (Deloitte 2018, p. 6). And it appears that Chinese-financed projects are awarded to Chinese companies, mostly SOEs.

Private participation in the BRI through public–private partnerships (PPPs) can contribute to affordable and superior quality infrastructure in three main ways (Taglioni and Gurara 2018). First, it can improve project selection and contribute to innovative solutions. Experienced private companies can identify infrastructure needs and come up with innovative ideas to meet them, which can be capitalized through bidding processes that are competitive, transparent, and eventually open to new ideas (World Bank 2017a). Second, where the incentive system is well aligned—say, by tying the private operator's revenue to a set of previously agreed-upon performance indicators—private participation improves operational efficiency. Third, to the extent that private capital is brought in and user fees are charged, private participation reduces the funding needs of government. If user fees are not charged, private participation only reduces the immediate funding needs of government, because in the long term the cost of the project must be covered by taxpayers.

But private participation in infrastructure is no panacea. Expectations have to be managed about the share of infrastructure projects that can be done through PPPs, the cost of PPP project preparation and implementation, and the extent to which they can reduce government funding requirements (Leigland 2018). Private capital accounted for 70 percent of the infrastructure investments with private participation in Eastern Europe and Central Asia in 2018, but only 55 percent in East Asia and Pacific. Governments or their state-owned banks, along with donors and multilateral development banks, account for the remaining financing (World Bank 2018c).[4]

Private sector participation goes beyond infrastructure. The potential gains of BRI interventions can be enhanced by a vibrant private sector that takes advantage of improved infrastructure and reduced trade costs. To increase private participation in the BRI, countries need to adopt complementary reforms to improve the business and investment climate facing potential investors, as elaborated below.

---

[2] State Assets Supervision and Administration Commission on October 30, 2018.

[3] http://finance.people.com.cn/n1/2018/1031/c1004-30372215.html.

[4] These figures are based on 198 projects, with investments totaling $45.7 billion, for which financing information was available. Information was not available for most projects in China, including the megaprojects.

**Figure 3.4:** Strength of protection of domestic investment laws and international investment agreements in 17 Belt and Road corridor economies

*Source:* Kher and Tran 2018.
*Note:* Scores are normalized to a 0–1 scale, with 1 the highest protection. The four countries that do not have a domestic investment law are Malaysia, Singapore, Sri Lanka, and Thailand.

## *Strengthening legal protection of investments*

Infrastructure projects tend to be large-scale, capital intensive, and with long development timelines–and thus present high risks for investors who are also particularly vulnerable to political and regulatory changes that can undermine profitability (OECD 2015). Investors will need to maneuver a diverse set of country laws and regulations, legal traditions, and court systems of varying effectiveness and capacities. That makes it essential for Belt and Road corridor economies to strengthen the legal protection of investment through unilateral and coordinated reform efforts.

Host countries can provide predictability by limiting arbitrary government interference and allowing dispute resolution and compensation when their obligations are violated. Both the legal rules (de jure) and their enforcement (de facto) matter. While investment protection is determined by a multitude of legal and regulatory instruments, domestic investment laws and international investment agreements are the most standard legal instruments. Kher and Tran (2018) review these laws and agreements in 21 corridor economies along the six overland corridors.[5] Cross-country variation is driven by differences both in standard treatment and the availability of recourse mechanisms (figure 3.4). Protection in international investment agreements can also be low because the network of BRI partners is small. In all investment laws reviewed, one finding stands out consistently: the low scores on transparency.

---

[5] Including 17 domestic investment laws and 648 IIAs, which include 616 bilateral investment treaties and 32 agreements with investment chapters.

**Figure 3.5:** Strength of investment protection in international investment agreements along selected BRI rail routes

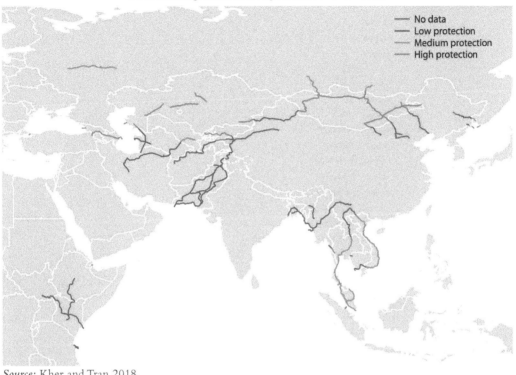

*Source:* Kher and Tran 2018.

Cross-country variation matters because many BRI connectivity projects along corridors cross different jurisdictions. An investor faces a different legal and regulatory framework whenever its project crosses a border—a challenge since it means investment protection varies along a single corridor. This happens at least for some of the rail routes (figure 3.5). Investment protection naturally is only as strong as it is in the weakest country.

Without effective enforcement, de jure legal provisions are mere promises on paper. Corridor economies vary in the strength of their judicial system and in their involvement in investor-state disputes (figure 3.6). Most dispute cases are in utilities and mining. The largest number of cases are in the electricity, gas, steam, and air conditioning supply subsector, followed by the extraction of crude petroleum and natural gas subsector. Most cases are based on alleged violations of core protection standards (Echandi 2018). The majority of the publicly disclosed cases in which the investor prevailed have been based on violation of fair and equitable treatment, closely followed by indirect expropriation (Kher and Tran 2018).

Access to effective mechanisms for dispute prevention and dispute settlement can improve the general level of enforcement in corridor economies, given that the BRI may generate a broad range of disputes—between private enterprises (including individuals),

## Figure 3.6

**a.** Investor–state dispute cases in 21 Belt and Road corridor economies

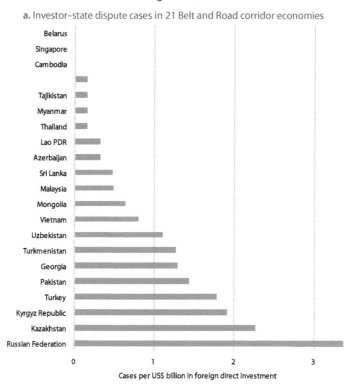

Cases per US$ billion in foreign direct investment

**b.** Rule of Law Index for 21 Belt and Road corridor economies

(Percentile rank on index)

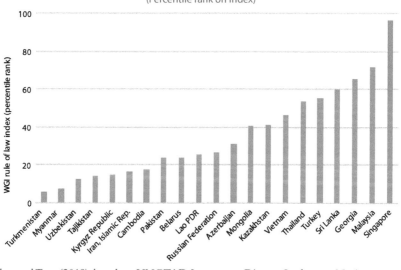

*Source:* **a.** Kher and Tran (2018), based on UNCTAD Investment Dispute Settlement Navigator. (http://investmentpolicyhub.unctad.org/ISDS). **b.** Kher and Tran (2018), based on World Bank World Governance Indicators. http://info.worldbank.org/governance/wgi/#reports.
*Note:* This index captures perceptions about the courts, judicial independence, the quality of contract enforcement, the fairness and speediness of judicial process, and the enforcement of property rights.

investor–state, and state–state. Several initiatives on investment-related dispute settlement mechanisms dedicated to the BRI have been explored, mostly covering commercial arbitration. For example, China has two international commercial courts dedicated to commercial disputes related to the BRI, and an International Commercial Expert Committee is expected to provide expert knowledge on mediation, arbitration, and litigation. Various dispute settlement options are being considered in other countries as well. For example, the Lahore-based Center for International Investment and Commercial Arbitration has a memorandum of understanding with the Hangzhou Arbitration Commission to serve as an arbitration center for disputes arising in the China–Pakistan Economic Corridor. Similarly, the China–Africa Joint Arbitration Centre was established in 2015 to resolve investment disputes between Chinese and African entities.

Initial efforts notwithstanding, greater clarity is needed in the dispute settlement mechanisms available to investors along the Belt and Road. Should a new comprehensive overarching mechanism be created? Or should there be greater consistency and harmonization in using the mechanisms already available? As corridor economies continue exploring options, dispute resolution mechanisms must be credible to be effective, suitable for the investor community, and recognized internationally. A tension stands between the benefits of a comprehensive mechanisms and the freedom of choice for courts, forums, procedural rules, laws, and languages.

## Supporting private sector development

Belt and Road corridor economies are highly heterogenous in the regulatory environment they provide for their private firms. Singapore and Hong Kong SAR, China, score 84 or 85 of 100 on the overall ease of doing business, while 19 other corridor economies score below 60. It takes 1.5 days to start a business in Singapore and Hong Kong SAR, China, but 99 days in Cambodia and 174 days in Lao PDR on the other extreme (figure 3.7).

Among the actions corridor economies are taking to improve their investment climate and private sector performance, special economic zones (SEZs), including industrial parks and other variations, have received particular attention (box 3.6). Despite such high-profile success stories as in China, SEZs have a decidedly mixed record. SEZ-related infrastructure investments in some countries became large fiscal drains that failed to attract investors, leaving "white elephants." And in some cases, investors have exploited SEZs to take advantage of tax breaks without delivering substantial employment or export earnings. In the big SEZ success stories, experimental policies have been piloted before being rolled out to the broader economy; and in the absence of political will to undertake reforms, SEZs acted as second-best environments and pressure valves to absorb excess labor (Farole 2017). The experience of SEZs in corridor economies helps identify the factors that allow these experiments to succeed.

**Figure 3.7:** Number of days to start a business in Belt and Road corridor economies

*Source:* World Bank Doing Business 2019 data.

**Box 3.6:** Special economic zones in the Belt and Road corridor economies

According to China's Ministry of Commerce (MOFCOM), as of October 2017, Chinese enterprises had developed 75 SEZs dubbed Overseas Economic and Trade Cooperation Zones (OETCZs) in 24 Belt and Road corridor economies of the 99 Chinese overseas zones. The number of registered enterprises within the zones reached 3,412, or 78 percent of the enterprises in all Chinese overseas zones. MOFCOM reports that 56 OETCZs in the corridor economies in September 2016 had a total investment of US$18.6 billion, output of US$50.7 billion, created 177,000 jobs, and contributed US$1.1 billion in taxes to the host countries. The zones are open to investors in the host country and from other countries.

So far, the performance of these zones has been mixed. Some are good performers, including the Long Jiang Industrial Park (Vietnam), Sino–Thai Rayong Industrial Park (Thailand), the Karawang Industrial New City (Indonesia), China–Egypt TEDA Suez Economic and Trade Cooperation Zone (Egypt), and Central European Trade and Logistics Cooperation Zone (Hungary). A common factor is the sound infrastructure and strong connectivity in the zones and surrounding areas. For example, the Long Jiang Industrial Park is only about 50 kilometers to Ho Chi Minh City center, Saigon seaport, and Hiep Phuoc seaport and about 35 kilometers to Bourbon port, conveniently connected through the newly built Ho Chi Minh City—Trung Luong Highway. The Sino-Thai Rayong Industrial Park is close to the Thai capital, Bangkok, and the deep-water port of Laem Chabang; and the TEDA Suez zone is 120 kilometers from the capital, Cairo, and only 2 kilometers from the most modern port in Egypt, the port of Sokhna, with easy access to 170 ports in the world. Other key factors include a stable and conducive macroenvironment, proper planning and industrial positioning based on local comparative advantages, the availability of skills, and a market-based sustainable business model.

Lagging zones face challenges in poor infrastructure on connectivity, risky macroeconomic and business environments, lack of commitment and support from the host governments, shortage of skills, difficulty in raising capital, and lack of operational experience and a sustainable business model. The China–Lao Mohan-Boten Economic Cooperation Zone suffers from skill shortages, especially for zone management, partially due to the poor macro environment in Lao PDR making it difficult to attract and retain talent. The Sino–Kazakhstan Horgos International Border Cooperation Center also took a long time to take off due to cultural and capacity gaps and the lack of a clear business model.

## 3.4 PROMOTING INCLUSIVENESS

Reduced trade costs will trigger aggregate welfare gains through a reallocation of resources across sectors and firms and the spatial concentration of economic activity within Belt and Road corridor economies. These effects can be associated with rising economic and spatial inequalities because workers are not fully mobile and are slow to adjust to new opportunities. Such immobility or slow adjustment calls for complementary policies that promote inclusiveness.

## Labor displacement and policies to speed adjustment

A reduction of trade costs imposes adjustment costs, especially in the short and medium runs. These costs may arise because of increased competition from Chinese products, which could challenge local industries. But the export sector in Belt and Road corridor economies, benefitting from improved access to China's vast market, could cushion such effects.

Bastos (2018) uses detailed bilateral trade data for the period 1995–2015 to assess the degree of exposure of corridor economies to China trade shocks. These effects are highly heterogeneous across corridor economies. Exposure to competition from China is higher in Hong Kong SAR, China; Indonesia; Malaysia; the Philippines; Thailand; and Vietnam. These economies source a relatively large share of imports from China and have export and production structures similar to China's. Further integration with China would likely produce stronger competitive pressures in final goods markets. Several other corridor economies are only weakly exposed to competition shocks associated with further integration with China. Bangladesh, the Islamic Republic of Iran, the Kyrgyz Republic, Mongolia, Myanmar, Tajikistan, and Timor-Leste source a sizable share of imports from China but are only weakly exposed to Chinese import competition in their own markets and have export structures that differ considerably.

For the Belt and Road corridor economies as a whole, total displacement over the baseline projected in 2030 is some 12 million workers, or 0.48 percent of the baseline labor force (table 3.3) (Maliszewska and van der Mensbrugghe 2018). This is a relatively small number, reflecting the assumption that the initiative will have a transitional phase. East Asia and Pacific is expected to lose agricultural employment of about 800,000, while South Asia would gain more than 4 million workers in agriculture. In East Asia and Pacific, 0.9 percent of the labor force is expected to switch jobs, followed by Sub-Saharan Africa with 0.6 percent, and the Middle East and North Africa with 0.5 percent. The Belt and Road corridor economies could see a net loss of almost 0.8 million agricultural jobs in 2030 relative to the baseline. The majority of this loss would be in China, though other countries such as Malaysia and Thailand would also see agricultural employment losses. Bangladesh, India, and Pakistan would see major increases in agricultural employment, as would Kenya and Tanzania.

Table 3.3: Labor displacement

| | Agriculture (thousands) | | Total displacement (thousands) | Percent of labor force |
|---|---|---|---|---|
| | Displaced– | Displaced+ | | |
| World total | −822 | 6,142 | 14,000 | 0.36 |
| Belt and Road corridor economies | −822 | 5,075 | 11,966 | 0.48 |
| Non–Belt and Road corridor economies | 0 | 1,067 | 2,033 | 0.15 |

*Source:* Maliszewska and van der Mensbrugghe 2019.

Corridor economies more exposed to competition should consider whether their social policies can deal with the adjustment costs associated with workers reallocating across occupations, sectors, and regions triggered by sector-specific competition and trade demand shocks. Countries more exposed to competition from China are likely to have more displaced workers and thus to face stronger adjustment costs. There is no one strategy for dealing with trade-induced adjustment costs (IMF, World Bank, and WTO 2017). The optimal policy depends on the shock, and on country attributes, and initial conditions. For example, facilitating geographic mobility may be especially important in larger economies or those in which such mobility has historically been low. General inclusive policies, notably social security and labor policies, including education and training, are options. Well-designed credit, housing, and place-based polices may also facilitate adjustment. And trade-specific adjustment programs may play a complementary role.

### *Territorial inequality and labor mobility*

Territorial inequalities risk frustrating investments and policy reforms, which are perceived as the source of the inequalities. In particular, poor internal labor mobility can exacerbate spatial differences in income. This section focuses on selected Central Asian countries, primarily because of data availability, but the issues are broadly applicable across BRI corridor economies. The largest spatial impacts from BRI investments are likely to be in Central Asia (including Kazakhstan, the Kyrgyz Republic, and Tajikistan), South Asia (Pakistan), and Sub-Saharan Africa (Kenya and Tanzania), which are relatively small economies in regions historically disconnected from world markets and with low domestic labor mobility. But even better connected East Asian countries—such as Lao PDR, Malaysia, Thailand, and Vietnam-have lagging areas with large shares of national populations.

In both Kazakhstan and Uzbekistan, spatial inequalities in welfare fall with declines in domestic migration costs (Lall and Lebrand 2019). Overall welfare increases as migration costs are reduced, highlighting the benefits of greater labor mobility for reducing spatial inequalities and improving overall welfare.

In Kazakhstan, workers at the periphery will benefit much less, as their access to the locations with high future opportunities are more limited than that of workers around the main urban centers of Almaty, Astana, Dzhambul, Karaganda, and Shymkent (figure 3.8a). These urban regions have expected utility from future opportunities 12 percent higher than in the periphery. Only around 2 percent of the population moves between regions in a given year, a much lower rate than in continent-size countries such as the United States (where 11 percent move) and Canada (14 percent). Greater domestic mobility would reduce the gap between the more isolated locations and the better connected areas.

In Uzbekistan, workers in western districts, with limited access to the locations with high future opportunities, will benefit much less than workers in eastern districts. The expected utility from future opportunities is 20 percent higher in the center of the country—in Jizzah,

Samarqand, Sirdaryo, Surxondaryo, and Tashkent (figure 3.8b). If mobility constraints were much lower, this gap would be reduced by two-thirds. Additional support for individuals in the most isolated locations could compensate for their lower access to future economic opportunities.

**Figure 3.8:** Barriers to labor mobility exacerbate spatial inequalities, reducing opportunities

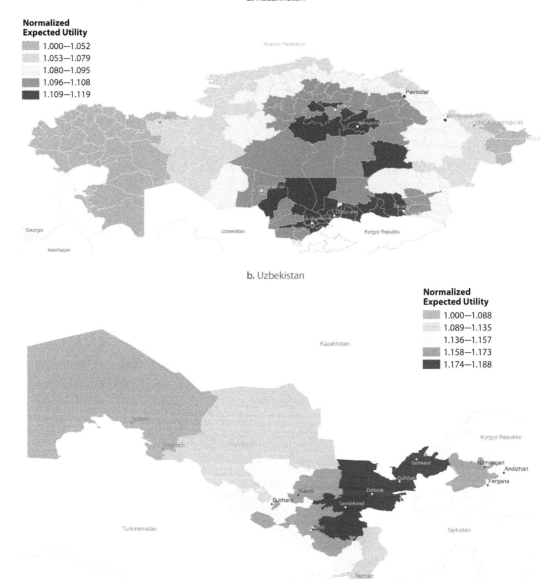

a. Kazakhstan

b. Uzbekistan

*Source:* Lall and Lebrand 2019.

Two sets of policy issues may need to be reconsidered to help with spatial labor mobility. First is the propiska systems of Central Asia, often referred to as "internal passport requirements," combined with strict rules for the place of residence where a person is officially registered. These systems have a long history in the region, predating even the restrictive Soviet system. Obtaining registration is particularly difficult in the largest cities (Ashgabat, Astana, Almaty, Bishkek, Dushanbe, and Tashkent). Since independence, propiska requirements have been used to limit internal migration, especially to slow migration to Ashgabat and Tashkent. But even the more relaxed requirements in Kazakhstan and the Kyrgyz Republic are very restrictive by global standards. Large populations live without registration in urban areas. But in most cases, persons living in a city without propiska registration cannot be officially employed there and are not authorized to use most government services, including healthcare and public education. Temporary propiska registration, available in some countries, still restrict a person's employment options and provide only limited permission to use public services.

Second, high and rapidly increasing housing prices (as in Almaty and Astana) and lack of rental housing make it difficult for migrants to move to cities. And limited land and property rights make it difficult for potential migrants to trade and sell assets in their home regions.

### *Other territorial policies*

Hubs can benefit from increased market potential, but investment and policy coordination failures can blunt the opportunities. Cities that could benefit from increased market access need policies that leverage local scale economies and investments that expand the delivery and quality of public goods and services for a growing population.

The Almaty city and region are well positioned to benefit from the connectivity improvements delivered by BRI (figure 3.9a) (Lall and Lebrand 2019; Reed and Trubetskoy 2019). Bishkek, Shimkent, Tashkent, and Urumqi (with total population of more than 8 million people) will all be within a 10-hour drive from Almaty (figure 3.9b). But translating this potential into tangible benefits requires taking coordinated action to address persistent national and local constraints–and revisiting the city's development strategy. Almaty is ready to capitalize on the BRI windfall, but the city and region will need to address substantial constraints, primarily to accommodate a growing population (Guha and Sivaev 2018). The city is reaching its growth limits, and land available for new developments is scarce.[6]

---

[6] According to an interview with Kazakh investment agency representatives, who conducted a survey of undeveloped lots in town.

**Figure 3.9:** Impact of BRI transport investments on Almaty

**a.** Estimated economic benefit captured in total rise in land values

**b.** Distance traveled from Almaty within a 10-hour
drive before BRI completion (in violet) and after BRI completion (in blue)

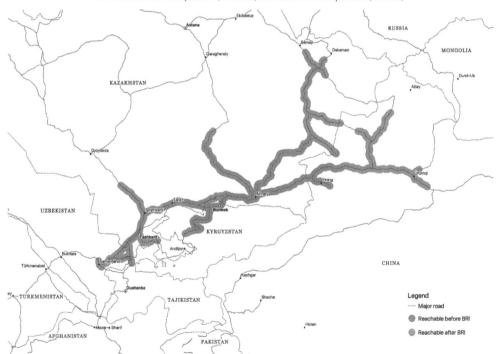

*Source:* Modeling by the World Bank.

A related problem is creating economic opportunities for migrants and ensuring that they have skills. A lot of additional labor can be absorbed in trade, local services, and tourism (so far a very small industry), but manufacturing and logistics can also be a source of mid-skill employment. The industrial zone is planning to pilot a training center that will allow companies operating in the zone to upskill workers and link directly to local educational institutes. This should benefit the growing population for the city and unlock urban competitiveness.

Limited remits of subnational governments and coordination failures across government tiers limit the local response to BRI initiatives, however. In Kazakhstan, the Almaty regional government is heavily restricted in what it can do to prepare for the BRI without the support of national government. Regions in Kazakhstan are responsible for 48 percent of public spending, one of the world's highest rates. This mostly reflects their vast responsibilities in service delivery, including healthcare and education. In practice, regions and local governments rely highly on national government for capital investments. And even though Almaty is the richest area in the country, it still relies on the national government for bigger interventions, such as the industrial zone and bypass road.

Complementary policies and investment can allow cities and subnational hubs to benefit from BRI investments:

- *Investments in the logistics industry.* Large-scale transport investments in and around a specific city can help turn it into a local transport and logistics hub. But for this to happen efficiently and effectively, targeted investments and upgrades to the logistics supply chain are required.

- *Land use policies and property rights.* An efficient land registration and land use regulation system—and an up-to-date cadaster—are prerequisites for a well-functioning urban land market, both for enabling investment and for providing for the local labor force. Land market constraints can also include restrictions on foreign ownership.

- *Improvements to infrastructure and municipal services.* The population influx associated with transport investments puts pressure on local infrastructure and municipal services. To help manage this, local governments can target investments in local transport networks and policies to improve housing affordability, such as tax incentives for affordable real estate development and reductions in residential zoning restrictions.

- *Skill development and small and medium enterprise development programs.* Investing in local human capital helps to attract new investment and service existing investments. By supporting local small and medium enterprises with business development and access to finance, local governments can augment and strengthen supply chains for larger local investments.

- *Investment promotion and use of anchor tenants.* Local government authorities can engage in proactive investment promotion, especially centered on anchor tenants for development zones, building long-term relationships with recognizable brand names to attract further investment.

# CHAPTER 4

## Managing the risks

BRI projects carry inherent risks common to large-scale infrastructure projects, heightened because of weak domestic institutions and poor economic fundamentals in many participating economies.

Given the scale of the BRI investments, fiscal risks are among the largest for countries and investors, particularly for countries with high debt burdens. Financing terms need to be clear, transparent, and understood—and in the context of fiscal frameworks that adhere to international standards. Governance risks for infrastructure projects are also high, and even higher for projects on the scale of many BRI investments. Open and transparent public procurement—incorporating appropriate audit and integrity functions as well as citizen accountability measures—are fundamental for these projects to succeed.

The BRI will also affect local populations and their environments. Pollution, deforestation, and environmental degradation can go hand in hand with the positive impacts of faster growth and increased trade. Governments must think strategically about how to mitigate potential negative impacts while also incorporating measures to make infrastructure greener and less intrusive.

## 4.1 MANAGING FISCAL RISKS

### *Fiscal risks*

BRI investments identified by news articles, Chinese institutions, and other data sources in the 70 Belt and Road corridor economies, excluding China, amount to US$575 billion (chapter 1). This total includes not only transport projects but all projects that are operating, under way, or planned. The BRI has the potential to accelerate the economic integration and development of a large number of countries. But the large cost of BRI projects raises concerns about the debt sustainability in some beneficiary countries, magnified by the poor information on the investment and financing terms of BRI projects and, for some corridor economies, by the lack of a comprehensive fiscal framework.

Information on the terms of financing of BRI-related projects is very sparse. Under the BRI, investment projects are likely to be structured as public investments or as public-private partnerships (PPPs), with one Chinese state-owned company as the foreign participating company. Financing is expected to be mainly foreign-currency denominated debt to a government, SOE, or private entity—or as foreign direct investment (with or without some form of guaranteed return). Interest costs and maturities of Chinese loan are on average more favorable than borrowing on market terms. Data reported by debtor countries to the World Bank suggest that most Chinese loans are concessional, but with terms that may not be the most favorable for LIDCs.[1] Most Chinese loans to LIDCs have fixed interest rates with a median rate of 2 percent, a grace period of 6 years, and a maturity of 20 years. Terms to LIDCs have been stable over time, corresponding to a median grant element of 40 percent. The median annual maturity of loans to EMEs fluctuates between 12 and 18 years, and the grace period between 3 and 5 years. A growing share of loans to EMEs have flexible interest rates, benchmarked to the 6-month LIBOR rate. Interest rates that Chinese lenders apply to LIDCs are on average more favorable than loans to EMEs but remain higher than those available from other creditors for countries at low and moderate risk of debt distress. The median loan from China fully disburses between 2.5 and 7.5 years from the year of commitment, in both LIDCs and EMEs. Yet, Chinese loans are often associated with other economic costs, such as those arising from collateralization, which are difficult to assess given limited availability of information.

Several countries with already elevated debt vulnerabilities are expected to benefit from significant BRI investments. Estimated BRI debt financing for all projects is expected to exceed 5 percent of GDP in four LIDCs at high risk of debt distress and in two LIDCs at moderate risk of debt distress (figure 4.1). Six more LIDCs, currently at low risk, are expected to receive sizable BRI investment. For three LIDCs (Cambodia, Tajikistan, and Timor-Leste), the estimated BRI-debt financing is expected to exceed the public or publicly guaranteed (PPG) debt-to-GDP ratio as of end-2016. Five EMEs in high scrutiny and two in low scrutiny are also expected to receive BRI debt financing amounting to more than 5 percent of GDP.

An analysis that looks at all BRI debt (not just transport related) shows that BRI investment financing could exacerbate existing debt vulnerabilities in a number of countries (Bandiera and Tsiropoulos 2019). Several BRI-eligible countries faced rising debt levels already prior to the BRI (chapter 1). In many of these countries, the average of past primary fiscal balances was far from the level required to stabilize the debt-to-GDP ratio in 2018. The growth impact of BRI investment in several countries is unlikely to be enough to prevent public debt from rising further. Estimates suggest that in 15 LIDCs and 10 EMEs receiving BRI investment, the growth required to stabilize the debt ratio is higher than the estimated growth associated with BRI investment in the short and medium terms.[2]

---

[1] The World Bank's Debtor Reporting System (DRS) was established in 1951. It captures detailed information at loan level for external borrowing of reporting countries using standardized forms. The primary objective is to provide the Bank with reliable and timely external debt information to assess a borrowing country's foreign debt situation, creditworthiness, and economic management; and conduct its country economic work and assess regional and global indebtedness and debt servicing problems. Data submitted by countries are entered into the DRS database, from which the aggregates and country tables are produced and published annually in the International Debt Statistics publication (successor to Global Development Finance and World Debt Tables). For additional information, see https://datahelpdesk.worldbank.org/knowledgebase/articles/381934-what-is-the-external-debt-reporting-system-drs.

[2] Bandiera and Tsiropoulos (2019) use two different methodologies to assess the impact of infrastructure investment on growth. First, a theoretical approach, based on Devadas and Pennings (2018), applies a constant elasticity production function to derive the marginal productivity of BRI investments. This model assumes that the impact of additional investment on growth declines as the public capital stock rises and a constant investment efficiency over the medium term. Second, Bandiera and Tsiropoulos (2019) draw on Calderon and Serven (2014) to quantify the impact of public infrastructure investment on growth, using econometric estimates suitable for dynamic panel data models and likely endogenous regressors.

**Figure 4.1:** Public debt and expected BRI debt financing
(Percent of GDP)

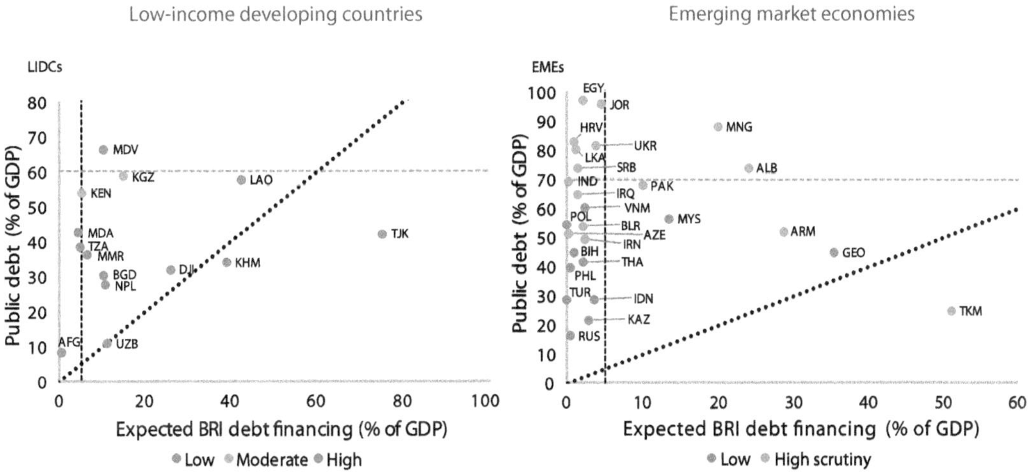

Low-income developing countries                    Emerging market economies

*Sources:* WEO, WIND Database, LIC DSF DSAs, and MAC DSAs.
*Note:* Assumes that (1) only BRI investments identified from 2016 to 2018 as under construction and planned would result in additional debt financing and (2) debt financing would amount to 40 percent of the cost of investment in the power, electricity, and mining sectors and 80 percent of the cost of the investment in transport and all other sectors.

Based on a sample of countries with detailed data, public debt of close to one-third of the corridor economies is expected to rise over the medium term as a result of the BRI. An assessment of debt vulnerability—based on debt levels, fiscal stance, expected growth, and expected BRI public debt financing—can identify corridor economies likely to further increase their public and publicly guaranteed debt-to-GDP ratios as a result of BRI financing in the medium term. This is relevant since BRI financing in the medium term is expected to be largely disbursed, but the long-term impact of BRI investment may not be entirely reflected in countries' growth. Of 43 economies analyzed, 12 are expected to increase their debt vulnerability as a result of BRI investment over the medium term (figure 4.2). Most of these 12 economies present vulnerabilities that predate the BRI. The seven LIDCs include four of the five LIDCs in the sample at high risk of debt distress and two of the three LIDCs in the sample assessed at moderate risk. Among five EMEs, four are considered high scrutiny countries, with an indebtedness ratio above 50 percent in 2018, and one a low vulnerability country, with public and publicly guaranteed debt expected to rise above 50 percent of GDP by 2023. [3]

Model-driven long-term simulations find that BRI investment would increase debt vulnerabilities only in two corridor economies, with an additional six countries sensitive to the

_____

[3] Given limited data availability, the analysis should be considered a preliminary exercise since it relies on several strong assumptions about BRI investments, their financing terms, their impact on growth, and the countries' fiscal stance. A more detailed analysis, ideally based on debt sustainability analyses of individual countries, would be needed to carefully assess the impact of the BRI on countries debt outlooks.

**Figure 4.2:** Projected status of Belt and Road corridor economies in 2023
(Percent of GDP)

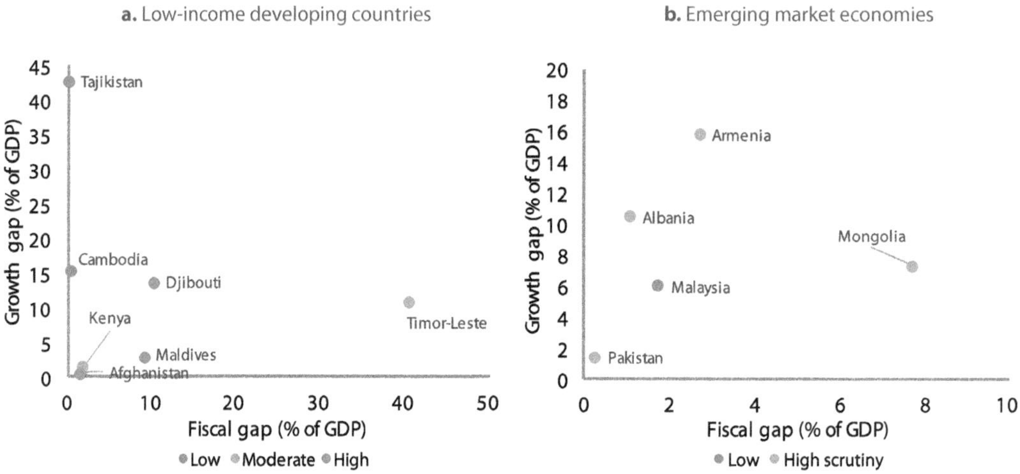

a. Low-income developing countries

b. Emerging market economies

*Source:* WEO, WIND Database, MAC DSAs, and LIC DSF DSAs.

terms of financing. Simulations have employed the result of the structural general equilibrium model used in chapters 2 and 3, to account for the full effect of trade-related infrastructure, policy reforms, and externalities on GDP (de Soyres et al. 2019). Simulations compared debt dynamics with respect to a scenario in which no BRI investment would take place and growth, primary balance and interest rate would be equal to their long-term historical averages. In the long term, debt dynamics are mainly driven by long-term drivers, and BRI investment would generally result in lower indebtedness in most countries—and would require adjustment to limit the build-up of debt vulnerabilities in only a handful of countries.

BRI investments may also add to fiscal risks, defined as the source of increased financial requirements that a government could face in the future. In corridor economies, governments are expected to contribute to the financing of BRI investment through direct borrowing or issuing debt guarantees (either from the central government, a government agency, an SOE, or a subnational entity). A significant share of BRI investments, especially in the energy sector, would involve private financing. In addition, significant policy corrections may be needed to stabilize public debt levels in some corridor economies. However, there is a risk that the need for a policy correction—in conjunction with elevated debt, large debt-financed investment, and weak fiscal institutions—could also increase fiscal risks (such as those stemming from guarantees or PPPs). Moreover, the possible materializing of cost overruns,[4] frequent in large infrastructure projects (box 4.1), may put additional pressures on the debt burden.

---

[4] Beyond those represented by explicit government guarantees, which are by definition included in public or publicly guaranteed debt.

Some authors also suggest that about a third of Chinese loans may be collateralized (Brautigam and Hwang 2016). In a collateralized loan, the borrower has pledged or sold a specific asset to the lender as security against repayment of the loan. The underlying collateral can take many forms, such as the assets of an SOE, physical commodities destined for export markets, or a future revenue stream. Certain types of collateralized borrowing can impair a government's ability to meet or reschedule its liabilities and introduce significant macro risks. In countries with weak public investment management frameworks, the availability of funds in the immediate term may also induce borrowing countries to invest in large-scale infrastructure projects based on their ability to secure financing, rather than on the priority accorded to such projects in the government's overall development strategy.

Corridor economies would also need to manage risks typical of megaprojects, which require investment of US$1 billion or more. Of the 45 corridor economies with identified investments, 36 have investments exceeding US$1 billion, with about half the total invested in energy and mining and a fourth in transport and shipping. These projects are highly likely to experience large cost overruns and severe delays, which could become large future liabilities for the governments of corridor economies (box 4.1).

---

**Box 4.1:** The risk of failure of megaprojects

Infrastructure megaprojects, those costing US$1 billion or more, are often considered crucial for the future of cities or countries. If done right, they create and sustain employment, contain a large element of domestic inputs relative to imports, improve productivity and competitiveness by lowering producer costs, benefit consumers through higher quality services, and improve the environment when infrastructure that is environmentally sound replace infrastructure that is not.

But their performance has been poor, with a consistent history of cost overruns (box table 1) for both private and public sector projects. Average cost overruns are of 96 percent for dams and 45 percent for railways (Flyvbjerg 2014). Only 1 to 2 of every 10 are delivered on schedule, and about the same share achieve the expected economic and social benefits, with demand often below expectations. Successful megaprojects, delivering the promised benefits on budget and on time, are then approximately 1 to 8 in every 1,000 projects (Flyvbjerg 2017).

Execution of megaprojects is often plagued by weakness in organizational design and capabilities, with actors changing over time and delivery methods reacting to unforeseen problems (often due to poor planning) and to stakeholders with competing interests (contractors eager to maximize payments and political sponsors to minimize costs). In addition, poor planning may impede input delivery and land acquisition or encounter other disputes, particularly in multicountry infrastructure. Despite the scale of the project, a single issue can block the implementation of the entire project and trigger penalties. Timely monitoring is also very difficult.

Megaprojects are prone to "slow fail" processes, making it difficult to avoid higher costs. At the planning stage, costs and timelines are systematically underestimated and benefits overestimated. The projects are often considered unique, with little attempt to learn from other projects. This is a mistake, for there is a lot to learn from experience.

**Table B4.1.1:** Cost overruns in selected infrastructure megaprojects

| Project | Cost overrun (%) |
| --- | --- |
| Suez Canal, Arab Republic of Egypt | 1,900 |
| Troy and Greenfield Railfoad, United States | 900 |
| Furka Base Tunnel, Switzerland | 300 |
| Verrazano Narrow Bridge, United States | 280 |
| Boston's Big Dig Artery/Tunnel Project, United States | 220 |
| Denver International Airport, United States | 200 |
| Panama Canal, Panama | 200 |
| Minneapolis Hiawatha Light Rail Line, United States | 190 |
| Humber Bridge, United Kingdom | 180 |
| Dublin Port Tunnel, Ireland | 160 |
| Montreal Metro Laval Extension, Canada | 160 |
| Copenhagen Metro, Denmark | 150 |
| Boston–New York–Washington Railway, United States | 130 |
| Great Belt Rail Tunnel, Denmark | 120 |
| London Limehouse Road Tunnel, United Kingdom | 110 |
| Brooklyn Bridge, United States | 100 |
| Shinkansen Joetsu High-Speed Rail Line, Japan | 100 |
| Channel Tunnel, United Kingdom–France | 80 |
| Karlsruhe–Bretten Light Rail, Germany | 80 |
| London Jubilee Line Extension, United Kingdom | 80 |
| Bangkok Metro, Thailand | 70 |
| Mexico City Metroline, Mexico | 60 |
| High–Speed Rail Line South, Netherlands | 60 |
| Great Belt East Bridge, Denmark | 50 |

*Source:* Flyvbjerg 2017.

## Policies and institutions to manage the risks

The assessment to identify potential debt vulnerabilities associated with BRI investments focuses on country-specific analysis and thus helps countries manage fiscal risks and benefit from increased investments without compromising debt sustainability:

- Countries in low scrutiny or low risk of debt distress, if not substantially increasing their indebtedness as a result of the BRI, would generally have the fiscal space to increase investment. However, it is important that projects are selected and implemented well to maximize development gains and that financial terms are appropriated and transparent.

• In addition to a careful project selection and evaluation of terms and available options of financing, countries that would increase their indebtedness should carefully evaluate the BRI's impact on their debt sustainability outlook and fiscal risks.

• Countries with limited or no fiscal space would need to limit the number of debt-financed projects, rely on grant or highly concessional financing, favor foreign direct investment over debt financing, and, if possible, increase public savings to finance additional investments.

Some countries that are expected to receive large BRI financing lack comprehensive and sound fiscal frameworks. According to the Public Expenditure Performance Assessment (PEFA), the fiscal framework of Belt and Road corridor economies is not, on average, worse than that of countries at the same level of development. But several economies expected to receive large BRI financing score insufficiently on the presence of unreported government operations, lack an adequate framework to monitor and manage fiscal risks, do not formulate a multiyear budget, and have opaque procurement practices.

BRI financing involves significant lending to SOEs and increased PPPs. For these reasons, most corridor economies would benefit from strengthening oversight of SOEs and PPPs and the corresponding regulatory frameworks. PPPs are widely used to design, finance, build, and operate large infrastructure projects. Proper regulatory systems and government capacity to plan, procure, and implement such projects are important to reap efficiency gains and to limit fiscal risks associated with large investments.

Since 2015, the World Bank Procuring Infrastructure PPPs (World Bank 2018d) has assessed the legal and regulatory quality to prepare, procure, and manage PPPs in client countries including 57 of the BRI host countries.[5] When benchmarked against recognized international good practices, BRI host countries score at 50 (range 0–100) in preparation of PPP projects, 66 in adoption of PPP procurement best practices, and 52 in PPP contract management. There is a significant room for improvement particularly in preparing PPP projects, where there is the largest variation among BRI host countries. Only 32 percent of the BRI host countries have a specific system for accounting PPP liabilities, and no more than 25 percent have a system to budget PPPs or report liabilities associated with PPP projects. Moreover, when preparing a project, only 21 percent of the BRI countries have a methodology in place to assess the fiscal risk associated with PPP project (World Bank 2018d).

Lack of transparency around the terms and size of BRI financing poses significant risks for borrowing countries and other creditors and, ultimately, for the success of the initiative. Debt transparency is critical for borrowers and creditors to make informed decisions, ensure efficient use of available financing, and safeguard debt sustainability. It is also important for

---

[5] The exercise was designed following the World Bank Doing Business methodology.

citizens to be able to hold governments accountable. In this context, it will be critical to build on past successful engagements with borrowing countries and the international creditor community, including China, while further enhancing coordination around sustainable lending practices and debt restructuring regimes.

To enhance the analysis of debt sustainability, fiscal risks, and debt reporting transparency, China has published a debt sustainability framework (BRI DSF) for low-income BRI countries at the 2nd Belt and Road Forum in April 2019. The BRI DSF is largely informed by the joint World Bank–IMF Debt Sustainability Framework for low-income countries. This tool is expected to be used on a voluntary basis to assess the debt sustainability outlook of BRI recipient countries. While the launching of the BRI DSF is a step in the right direction, its effectiveness depends on whether and how participating countries and financial institutions will use it, the realism of the assumptions underpinning the analysis and the comprehensiveness of data used for calculating public debt indicators and contingent liabilities.

Other tangible actions that the government of China could implement to increase transparency and help debtor countries and creditors correctly estimate risks from public debt financing of BRI investments include adopting a comprehensive database of BRI projects, inclusive of financing terms, and expected new lending; adhering to a borrowing country's primary and secondary legislation establishing the authority to borrow and issue guarantees on behalf of the government; ensuring that the amount of financing appropriately reflects the value of the BRI projects; and adopting publicly available templates for financing arrangements under the BRI, while refraining from using confidentiality clauses. Finally, China could make public its participation in debt restructuring operations. It would also benefit from having a debt restructuring framework in place, conducive to providing required relief in a timely fashion and enabling China to participate in a collaborative approach with other creditors, when appropriate.

## 4.2 MANAGING GOVERNANCE RISKS

### *Public procurement*

For governments to reap the benefits of BRI projects, procurement should be open, transparent, and competitive—with awards going to the firms best placed to execute a project, regardless of their ownership or nationality. The regulations and practices of both host countries and the major provider of financing for BRI projects, China, are relevant in assessing what is being done in BRI projects. They are also relevant in determining how BRI-related procurement can conform more closely to international good practices. Following good practices is important for host borrowing countries, as they have a strong interest in ensuring that they obtain the best value for money. It is also important for China and the financial institutions that finance BRI projects, since it can help ensure the integrity and financial performance of projects.

Comprehensive and comparable cross-country data permitting analysis of BRI-related procurement do not exist (Ghossein, Hoekman, and Shingal 2018). The limited publicly accessible information suggests that Chinese suppliers/contractors win the majority of BRI projects. Data compiled by the Center for Strategic and International Studies for a limited sample of BRI projects for which this can be determined (see below) suggest that more than 60 percent of Chinese-financed BRI projects are allocated to Chinese companies. While Chinese firms are competitive and often are lower cost suppliers than non-Chinese firms, their dominance in BRI projects reflects policy as well as a willingness to invest in projects and areas that firms of other nationality may find too risky or challenging.

The source of financing has been a major determinant of how BRI projects are allocated to contractors. It has been estimated that about half of the financing for BRI projects (comprising outstanding loans or equity investment) has been provided by China's big four state-owned commercial banks. China Development Bank, the Export-Import Bank of China, and the Silk Road Fund have provided much of the rest. Financing by these entities involves both explicit and implicit preferences for Chinese suppliers, reflecting the fact that financing often has a concessional or preferential element as well as policy objectives that restrict the financing to Chinese contractors (Zhang and Gutman 2015).

The scope for enhancing foreign and local participation depends on the processes China and host countries use to define procurement needs and award contracts. To date, much of the awarding of contracting in BRI projects has gone through Chinese policy banks. In practice, the policy banks require borrowers to include the bank in the procurement process, including bidding and tendering activities. More broadly, foreign investment by Chinese enterprises is subject to approvals by Chinese government bodies such as the National Development and Reform Commission, the Ministry of Commerce, and the State-owned Assets Supervision Commission of the State Council. The ministry has a mandate to coordinate delivery of large projects in partner countries, working with relevant ministries, policy banks, and relevant SOEs. For projects that have a concessional finance element, the ministry has a mandate to oversee the associated procurement processes, creating opportunities for it to influence them (Hoare, Hong, and Hein 2018).

In itself, there is nothing remarkable in earmarking the award of BRI projects financed by Chinese entities to Chinese firms. Other countries do the same. Financing from national export–import banks or export credit guarantee institutions generally is earmarked for national companies, given the preferential or concessional nature of the associated financial support. The question is whether this is good practice. In the development finance context, many countries have agreed that the answer is no. This is reflected in the 2005 Paris Declaration on Aid Effectiveness calling on donor countries to move away from tying aid to sourcing goods and services from national firms.

A comparison of Belt and Road corridor economies, both as a single group and by World Bank region, against all 180 economies included in the Benchmarking Public Procurement database, reveals that corridor economies do not stand out as having public procurement processes much different from non–Belt and Road countries. In areas such as open tendering, online procurement, information requests, evaluation criteria, and promotion of competition, most corridor economies fall in line with international practices. But the variation among corridor economies is wide in several other essential areas of procurement—notably in the participation of foreign firms, the preference for local bidders, the management and modification of contracts, and complaint review mechanisms. Restrictions on participation by foreign firms in procurement opportunities is common in many countries. In almost all corridor economies, foreign firms are eligible to submit bids in response to calls for tender, but there may be restrictions on the type or size of procurement contracts, as in 40 percent of corridor economies.

The underlying goal motivating giving preference to domestic firms over foreign firms in corridor economies is usually a desire to use government resources to support domestic employment, investment, and learning. Granting a preference to local bidders— as by requiring procuring entities to grant a contract to a local firm if the bid does not exceed the lowest foreign bid by a specified percentage (often 15 percent)—is a common domestic preference scheme. Awarding contracts to local firms may have efficiency benefits by allowing firms to realize scale economies but it also comes at a cost. Many countries provide some preferential treatment to domestic firms through their legal framework, but with considerable variation (figure 4.3).

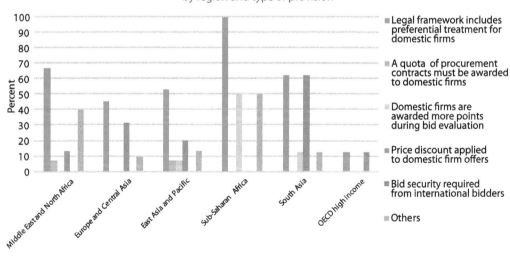

**Figure 4.3:** Belt and Road corridor economies where domestic preference provisions exist, by region and type of provision

*Source:* World Bank Benchmarking Public Procurement 2017 database (Ghossein, Hoekman, and Shingal 2018).
*Note:* Missing bars mean zero percentage of countries where domestic preference provisions exist.

## *Options for moving forward*

Efforts to improve procurement practices can follow three tracks—by BRI host countries, by China, and multilateral international agreements.

BRI hosts. A push to use host country procurement systems can be considered in instances where these systems adhere to recognized core principles such as transparency, efficiency, integrity, economy, value for money, and fit-for-purpose. In practice, these may not fully conform to international good practice. A first step could be to use diagnostics pertaining to national procurement system readiness with pre-tendering due diligence before deciding which procurement rules to apply. One possible way to enhance transparency and generate more information on BRI procurement is to mobilize resources to document the practices for awarding projects across countries. Greater transparency and the ability to assess the process of procurement associated with BRI projects would have the added benefit of facilitating future co-financing of projects with multilateral development agencies or other financing sources. A BRI-wide platform to encourage monitoring and provision of feedback by procuring entities can support learning and identify areas to improve practices.

China. The most straightforward path for China would be a unilateral decision that BRI projects financed by public Chinese entities would use international good practices for competition and transparency. First-best would be to specify that all Chinese-financed BRI projects exceeding a certain threshold value would employ international competitive bidding. Doing so could build on the scope that reportedly already exists in China's government procurement legislation: not to apply "buy Chinese" requirements in cases where goods and services are procured for use outside China.

Another option would be for BRI projects above a threshold value to be awarded through open national competition among Chinese companies, including foreign-invested enterprises. This may be second-best from an economic efficiency perspective, as it is not necessarily the case that China-domiciled firms will offer the best price-quality at all times. But it would be an improvement over limited or selective tendering. A third option, which does not entail any change to current processes and procedures (see below) would be to put in place (multilateral) systems to enhance the transparency of BRI procurement processes, including through regular reporting on tenders issued, number of bids received, and other procedural dimensions of project procurement.

International agreements. It can be difficult for governments to consistently apply procurement procedures that are open, transparent, and competitive. Political economy pressures invariably arise that may impede implementing international good practices or applying the processes specified in national laws and regulation. Multilateral cooperation among corridor economies can help to provide potential solutions—or elements of solutions. Joint investment in mechanisms to generate information could allow analysis of processes and resulting outcomes. And using international agreements, such as the WTO Government Procurement Agreement, could promote the use of transparent, competitive procurement practices.

A basic takeaway is that having better information about the public procurement processes associated with BRI projects would benefit all parties participating. The absence of comprehensive and comparable data makes it difficult to determine the effect of applied policies and processes on outcomes. Better knowledge of procurement would help in assessing the impacts of BRI projects, both in the construction phase and thereafter, and in evaluating the effectiveness of procurement processes in attaining value for money.

## *Corruption*

One of the most common governance risks in infrastructure projects is corruption—the abuse of public office for private gain. Perceptions of bribery are higher in construction and public works than any other sector, including the arms industry and oil and gas sectors, according to the Transparency International 2011 Bribe Payers Index. Corruption in transport projects can account for 5 percent to 20 percent of transaction costs (Kenny 2006).

**Table 4.1:** Definitions and example of corrupt practices in the infrastructure (transport) sector

| Corrupt activity | Definitions and examples |
| --- | --- |
| **Bribe** | Payment to a government official for any type of favor. Bribes are paid by firms to be short-listed or prequalified, to win contracts, to approve contract amendments and extensions, to influence auditors, to induce site inspectors to compromise their judgment regarding quality and completion of civil works, and to avoid cancellation of contracts for poor performance. |
| **Kickbacks** | Payment made by a successful bidder to a third party as a result of an arrangement made prior to bidding. This is typically regarded as a share of proceeds from a bid that has been padded sufficiently to cover the kickbacks. |
| **Collusion** | Agreements among bidders to manipulate the bidding process or its results in a manner that is mutually satisfactory. Public officials may orchestrate or be involved in collusion in return for a bribe. Collusion often involves bid rigging (see below). |
| **Bid rigging** | Actions that influence a bid price in a noncompetitive way to achieve a prearranged objective. All forms of bid rigging include some type of information or procedural asymmetry to tip the scale in favor of a contractor or consortium. Two common forms are manipulation of bid specifications and sole-source contracts, both of which unfairly exclude competition. In bid rigging involving collusion, parts of a bid may be deliberately raised in order to create a losing bid. he winning bid may be set above the known cost estimate ("highball") in order to finance kickbacks after award. In noncollusive bid rigging, contractors may submit a "lowball" bid, where the price is set low to win the contract, only to be increased after the contract award through change orders or addenda, often with the help of officials. |
| **Fraud** | Illicit documentary practices to subvert qualification requirements, such as commercial registration or financial capacity, or to cover up poor performance and corrupt practices, such as billing for work never performed, failing to meet contract specifications for road construction, and inflated billing for goods and services, among others. Fraud by project officials includes diverting project assets such as computers or vehicles, documenting "ghost employees," and setting up front companies (to create the illusion of competition or conceal the identity of the principal owners or beneficiaries beneficiaries for taxation avoidance, usually working in concert with selected complicit firms). |

*Source:* World Bank 2007.

Infrastructure sector corruption can include improper influence in budgeting and choosing projects and extracting rent in return for a carriage permit, construction contract, lease, or concession (World Bank 2007). Administrative corruption, which can occur at all levels of public service, usually includes an explicit transaction. State capture, by contrast, is usually indirect, as when policies benefit specific firms. Procurement and contract management are the two processes most vulnerable to corruption (table 4.1).

Corruption in infrastructure is widespread across the world, including in developed countries. Cartels of contractors agreeing on which firm would win road contracts in the Netherlands have led to a loss of US$500 million per year (Doree 2004). But the risk of corruption correlates closely with the level of development. This is because combating corruption is fundamentally about addressing poor governance and less developed countries more often than not face greater challenges in terms governance and rule of law. Subnational allocation of Chinese development finance projects to Africa over 2000–12 also suffered from corruption (Isaksson and Kotsadam 2018).

The latest Corruption Perception Index (CPI) scores suggest that the perceived corruption in Belt and Road corridor economies is higher than the global average and is highest among lower-middle- and low-income corridor economies (figure 4.4). There is also a positive correlation between CPI and rule of law (figure 4.5). Countries that are perceived to be low on corruption tend to have stronger rule of law probably because weaker investigative and judicial capacity means that fewer cases of corruption are detected and even fewer are likely to be solved and prosecuted.

**Figure 4.4:** Corruption Perception Index scores for Belt and Road corridor economies, 2017

**Figure 4.5:** Relationship between CPI and Rule of Law Index for 50 Belt and Road corridor economies, 2017

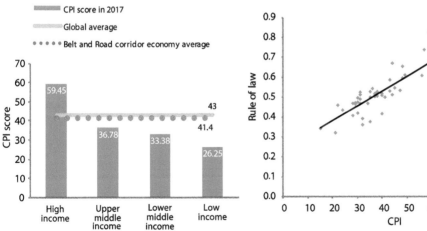

*Source:* Analysis by the World Bank using data on CPI from Transparency International.
*Note:* CPI scores range from 0 to 100 with 0 indicating high perceived corruption and 100 indicating low perceived corruption.

*Source:* Analysis by the World Bank using CPI data from Transparency International and rule of law data from the World Justice Project (2018).
*Note:* Rule of law scores range from 0 to 1 with 0 indicating weak perceived rule of law and 1 indicating strong perceived rule of law.

To reduce corruption in the infrastructure sector through better monitoring, reporting, and enforcement, supply-side measures can be addressed by governments and demand-side measures by public accountability instruments. Supply-side measures include:

- *Audits.* The BRI could provide an opportunity to develop common audit standards and to strengthen supreme audit and related institutions. Five types of audits are commonly implemented to reduce corruption and improve accountability: financial (periodic inspection of accounts); technical (periodic inspection of assets and services provided with the funds); fiduciary (comprehensive review of an implementing agency's procurement, financial management, and project management processes); procurement review (monitoring all procurement related practices); and third-party monitoring.

- *Construction Sector Transparency Initiative (CoST).* A multistakeholder initiative with 15 participating countries spanning four continents, CoST works with governments, industry, and local communities. By increasing transparency and accountability, it helps countries deliver better value from public infrastructure investment.

- *Red flags.* A set of indicators can alert officials to potential corruption during the infrastructure project cycle (Alexeeva, Queiroz, and Ishihara 2008). Not necessarily an indication of fraud, the alerts encourage officials to recognize and further track areas of potential vulnerability (Sieber 2014).

- *Integrity pacts.* An integrity pact is an agreement to refrain from corrupt acts between governments and contractors, and to sanction noncompliance during the tender process and the life of the contract. Corridor economies could use the pacts to improve the behavior of procurement officials and potential bidders. They also include demand-side elements, such as community monitoring tools. The pacts have been adopted successfully in large-scale government contracts in several Latin American countries, including Argentina, Colombia, Ecuador, and Mexico (Howkins 2013).

- *Information power.* The BRI could use information and communications technology to increase transparency in projects. Information includes guidelines, Internet-based tools, computerized applications for procurement, procurement monitors, and independent procurement agents. Information on assets, costs, and performance provides evidence that facilitates accountability and transparency. Tools like e-procurement can help achieve effective procurement and contract management. One of the major advantages of such a web-based system is that the same information is available to all participants. For such systems to flourish, the coverage, reliability, and security must be adequate, and the literacy of the industry sufficient for the information to expand (not limit) competition.

Measures on the demand side include:

- *Community monitoring.* Community monitoring is based on the principle that non-state actors can strengthen public accountability, improve governance, reduce inefficiencies, and combat corruption. Corridor economies can use it to improve accountability at a particular stage in the project cycle.

- *Citizen report cards.* The report cards can improve governance of projects by providing systematic feedback from users of public services. They can provide a rigorous and proactive agenda for communities, civil society organizations, and local governments to engage in a dialogue with infrastructure providers to improve projects (ADB 2007).

## 4.3 MANAGING ENVIRONMENTAL AND SOCIAL RISKS

### Direct and indirect environmental risks

The Belt and Road Initiative poses a wide range of environmental risks. Some projects have easily identifiable and measurable impacts such as energy projects' greenhouse-gas emissions. Others, such as transportation infrastructure, due to their vast geographic reach, generate more complex and potentially more extensive environmental risks.

Impacts include both direct impacts of the infrastructure and construction, and indirect impacts resulting from firm responses to new routes (Losos et al. 2018). Risks vary considerably between macro BRI projects and along micro sections of routes-according to local conditions, the type of infrastructure (rail versus road), and the quality of mitigation. Environmental impacts are also integrally related with social impacts (discussed next).

Direct BRI impacts include pollution from traffic, topographical and hydrological damage, and the alteration of habitats at the expense of biodiversity. For traffic pollution, the BRI should induce greater traffic along its routes, raising air and noise pollution. But many routes have electric-powered rail, tending to lower air pollution and greenhouse gas emissions (compared with road and air transport),[6] and noise pollution (compared with roads).[7] To the extent "greener" rail transport substitutes for previous road and air journeys, pollution may be reduced. This is particularly salient for the BRI, which tends to follow existing transport routes, making substitution more likely.

For topographical and hydrological damage, many routes pass through steep terrain, while rail and particularly high-speed rail are constrained to fairly straight paths, and less easily routed around topographical and hydrological barriers. Related risks include landslides, flooding, soil erosion, sedimentation in rivers, and interruptions of water courses. For some portions of the BRI, at-risk populations are large-such as Myanmar, where 25 million inhabitants downslope from two proposed BRI road projects are vulnerable to any increased sedimentation and induced flooding (Helsingen et al. 2018).

---

[6] Impacts on air pollution and greenhouse gases depend on the energy mix where electricity is generated. If electricity is produced by high-polluting coal-fired power stations, global warming impacts, as well as impacts around these power stations, may be large.

[7] Due to the lower frequency of trains.

Road and rail also affect biodiversity by fragmenting and altering species' habitats and by preventing animal movement. These barriers split populations and reduce genetic diversity in breeding, particularly for migratory and nomadic species. In addition, roads and rail lines change habitats along their edges, with impacts on species competition and survival. Changes in wind intensity, pollution, light, and noise along a road or railway may be subtle but can tip species competition in favor of more "edge-adapted" species; these tend to be less local, more resilient high breeders (weedy species), while endemic and vulnerable species suffer. Edge effects can be felt as far as 1,500 meters from a highway (Bruschi et al. 2015) and for the BRI are expected to extend at least a kilometer into adjacent roadside habitats in most cases (Benítez-López, Alkemade, and Verweij 2010; Ibisch et al. 2016). Edge effects are especially pronounced in tropical ecosystems (Goosem 2015), making the China–Indochina Peninsula Economic Corridor especially vulnerable. Edge effects of rails versus roads are inadequately studied, but expected to be somewhat less, given the narrower width of rail footprints and the lower frequency of traffic.

Risks from fragmentation and edge effects are reduced when (as is common in the BRI) corridors follow preexisting routes. Where the BRI merely improves existing routes, habitats are not newly fragmented, and edge effects are not newly created (though they may be changed or enhanced). But portions of proposed BRI routes create new routes through intact frontier landscape and pass through vulnerable or protected areas.

The greatest impacts of the BRI may not be these direct impacts of the infrastructure and traffic, but indirect impacts of improved accessibility on the location and production decisions of firms and households. Transport routes tend to raise the attractiveness of locations they connect, making densification along BRI corridors likely. This can take many forms, however, including dispersion toward new and emerging centers, or increased concentration in existing major centers. The impacts are often hard to predict, not varying directly with the extent of connectivity achieved or the balance of complementary advantages and disadvantages along routes (Duranton and Venables 2018). Location responses also depend on the type of infrastructure—for instance, high-speed rail tends to have few entry and exit points, located in major preexisting settlements, while lower-tier roads or rail have more access points, and thus opportunities for dispersion.

Indirect environmental impacts can be both positive and negative. Negative impacts are clearer, through increased emissions (see box 4.2) or in opening frontier locations to development (not just new settlement, but particularly high-cost activities like logging and illegal wildlife trade). But impacts can also be positive, as corridors encourage densification of settlement and production in a switch to off-farm activities that support rural land consolidation and restoration (Kazcan 2016). And broad income growth can reduce the environmental impacts of production and consumption through Environmental Kuznets Curve effects. These impacts tend to depend on prior development:

• Within highly developed (and deforested) regions such as Bangladesh, southwest China, and parts of Cambodia and Kazakhstan, not much vulnerable biodiversity and natural

**Figure 4.6:** BRI road and rail projects—operating, under construction, planned—in relation to biodiversity risks

**a.** Conservation International's biodiversity hotspots

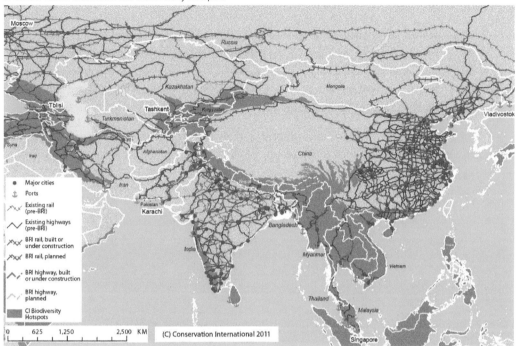

**b.** China–Indochina Peninsula Economic Corridor intact frontier landscapes and protected areas

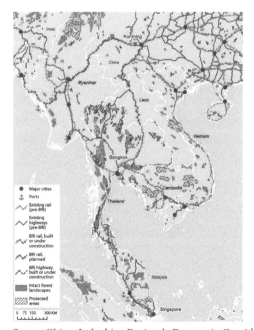

**c.** China–Indochina Peninsula Economic Corridor hotspots of biodiversity endemism for threatened species

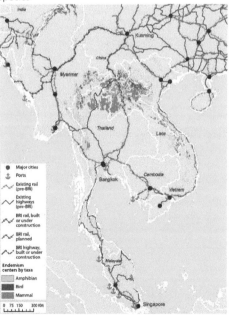

*Source:* China–Indochina Peninsula Economic Corridor hotspots are based on Li, Fan, and Wu 2017.

forest remain, leaving risks low. Here, positive environmental impacts as described above are more likely; similar positive dynamics have been observed for road construction along relatively populated, and already largely deforested, areas in India and China.[8]

• Projects in areas of medium development present higher risks. These represent the frontiers of transformation, where lower transport costs may push costs of settlement, logging, and so on over the margin of profitability.[9] The China–Indochina Peninsula Economic Corridor (CIPEC) and China–Mongolia–Russia Economic Corridor (CMREC) are among the most at-risk, with large areas facing deforestation in the past 15 years.

• In regions with low prior development and deforestation, such as eastern Russia and northwest Thailand, the short-term effects of BRI road or rail projects may be small; their

**Figure 4.7:** BRI road and rail projects—operating, under construction, planned—in relation to biodiversity risks

a. Belt and Road corridor economies' forest cover, forest loss, and forest gain

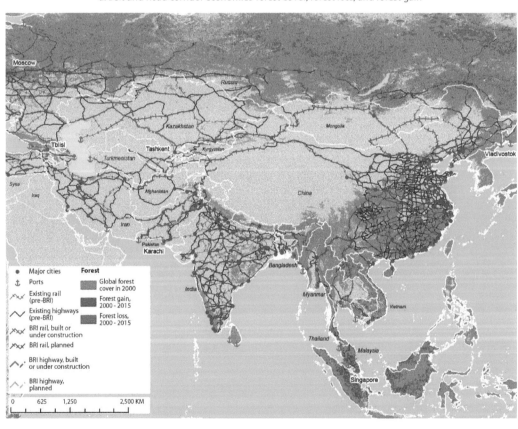

---

[8] Evidence for India from Asher, Garg, and Novosad 2017 and Kaczan 2016. Evidence for China from Deng et al. 2011.

[9] This reflects impacts of road building in Latin America, where investments in "medium" deforested and developed locations was associated with higher deforestation.

**b.** China–Indochina Peninsula Economic Corridor forest cover, forest loss, forest gain, and protected areas.

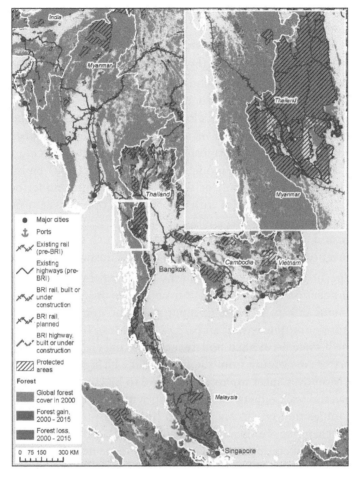

*Note:* Inset shows proposed BRI Burma Rail Nam Tok–Thanbyuzayat project

"frontier" nature implies higher costs and other barriers to development and exploitation. But degradation of such intact frontier landscapes is more harmful due to their important ecosystem functions, while in the long term there is greater uncertainty about how firms and households may respond to higher accessibility and the dynamic changes this induces.

Design choices about BRI routes and complementary policies will have a large impact on the final environmental costs. They include choices between alternative routes at macro and micro levels, transport modes (such as road versus rail), and a host of possible restoration, mitigation, and offsetting activities. Now is an opportune time to invest the small amounts needed to map environmentally vulnerable and valuable areas along the BRI and conduct social cost–benefit analyses to guide planners toward win-win scenarios. Implementing recommendations from social and environmental cost–benefit analysis will, in many cases,

**Box 4.2:** Impact of BRI transport infrastructure on emissions

The effect of BRI transport projects on emissions are low at the global level, but they may be sizable for specific countries given the changes in economic activity and the composition of production (Maliszewska and van der Mensbrugghe 2019).

The CGE model tracks the emissions of 14 gases. Four are the greenhouse gases (GHGs)[1] that are most linked with radiative forcing and global warming. The remaining 10 are mostly local pollutants with potentially significant health effects—but can also interact with the GHGs and have an impact on climate change. For example, sulfur dioxide in the atmosphere lowers radiative forcing and thus acts to cool the atmosphere. In the model, carbon dioxide ($CO_2$) emissions emanate exclusively from the combustion of fossil fuels—thus the model does not track changes from land use changes (as with deforestation) or process emissions (say, from cement manufacturing). The remaining 13 gases are generated from intermediate and final demand for goods and services, factor use (such as land in rice production, or herds in livestock), and such output as methane emissions from landfills).

The change in the pattern of emissions generated by the BRI scenarios will reflect a constellation of factors that can be broken into scale effects (changes in GDP), technique effects (changes in input mix), and composition effects (changes in the structure of output within and across countries). Technique effects are likely to remain small since no explicit policies are targeting emissions—the only changes in relative prices are coming from the trade policy changes, including those linked to the BRI. Moreover, most inputs are assumed to be consumed in fixed quantities. All else equal, the scale effects should line up with increases in GDP on a country basis. The composition effects are likely to be large as policies engendered by the BRI lead to changing comparative advantage with major changes in both the internal and external composition of output. These are not necessarily easy to trace in a modeled economy with many sectors and countries. If production moves to relatively clean sectors and countries, the composition effects may counteract the scale effects, or vice versa.

$CO_2$ emissions go up worldwide by around 0.3 percent, but there is considerable heterogeneity across countries and regions as highlighted (figure B4.2.1). The reasons vary. In Cambodia, the increase in output is very large in all three transport sectors. By contrast, Lao PDR sees a more modest increase in transport, around 5 percent, and fairly substantial increases in the output of leather goods, chemicals, rubber and plastics, and fabricated metal products. The Kyrgyz Republic is more similar to Cambodia, with large increases in the transport sector. China, on the other end of the spectrum, sees modest output declines in a number of sectors including air transport, chemicals, rubber, and plastics, and pulp and paper.

---

[1] Also referred to at times as the Kyoto gases as they were targeted in the Kyoto Protocol Agreement, signed in 1997.

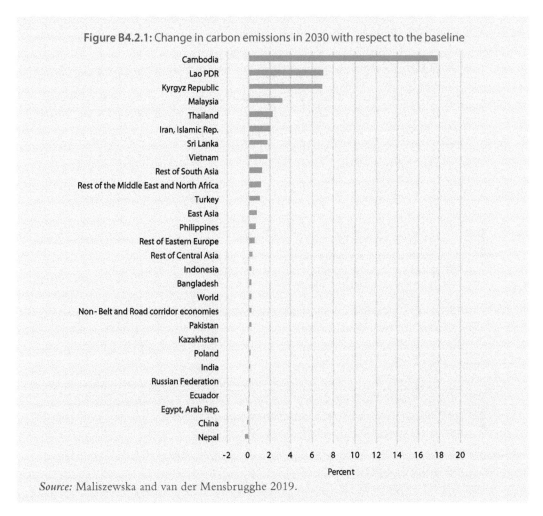

**Figure B4.2.1:** Change in carbon emissions in 2030 with respect to the baseline

*Source:* Maliszewska and van der Mensbrugghe 2019.

require improved institutional capacity among implementing agencies in BRI corridor countries, as well as from some Chinese financiers.

These environmental assessments can be undertaken at the corridor level and the project level (Losos et al. 2018). A BRI corridor environmental and social assessment would focus on the entire transportation corridor, taking advantage of the scale and connectivity of the BRI to address the cumulative direct and indirect risks from these projects. Such strategic assessments would involve a synthesis of existing data, studies, and information and would be strengthened through mechanisms to involve stakeholders and improve public transparency. Based on the project and potential impacts, design and assessment of individual projects can consider how to address the issues identified. Coordination across countries and implementing partners should work to ensure that methodologies employed in environmental and social assessments are consistent so that cumulative impacts can be considered and managed. Other specific actions to mitigate environmental risks are summarized in table 4.2. These actions are compatible with the World Bank's Environmental and Social Framework (box 4.3).

**Table 4.2:** Options for mitigating environmental risks

**Avoid**
Plan routes to avoid vulnerable environments.[a]
- Identify alternative route options that avoid the sensitive areas.
- Conduct a social cost–benefit analysis (considering economic, environmental, and social impacts) to guide selection between alternative routes. This analysis should consider transboundary impacts to mitigate contamination of invasive species, contamination of water resources, protection of cultural heritage and other intangible heritage, contaminated land, landscape, associated facilities, or linked projects.
- This should be done at the micro level, for large portions of the BRI, and for the BRI as a whole, to account for the interdependence of locations, investment impacts, and affected environments.

**Reduce**
Mitigate impacts through environmentally conscious engineering and complementary policy. Options include:
- Wildlife crossings (bridges and underpasses, with mechanisms to "funnel" wildlife to crossing), sound barriers, pointing lights downward to reduce light pollution, retention of trees, timing construction to avoid important times for animal migration or mating.
- Tunnel–bridge–tunnel engineering to reduce landslide and erosion risks.
- Regulation, enforcement, and incentives to reduce deforestation, poaching, and vulnerable species trade. This may include the creation of protected areas near transport corridors, addressing weaknesses in enforcement capacity, and making incentive/compensatory payments to landlords or local governments in return for maintaining forests and ecosystems. Protected areas should be coordinated along the BRI, to ensure that they reduce, rather than displace, harmful activity.
- Apply social cost–benefit analyses in selecting transport options (road categories, rail versus roads, electric versus standard rail, regulation on vehicle emissions and maintenance. These raise the case for favoring rail over roads-particularly high-speed electric-due to lower pollution, and reduced encroachment on frontier landscapes due to fewer access points and their concentration in already dense cities.

**Restore**
Take remedial action to repair damage inflicted by the construction process. For example:
- Stabilize damaged slopes.
- Replant vegetation.
- Repair disrupted waterways or wetlands.

**Offset**
Compensate for environmental damage that cannot be avoided, reduced, or restored, through investments in off-site locations that ensure net neutral or net positive environmental outcomes overall. Internationally-recognized offset programs offer standards by which BRI projects could evaluate themselves.[b] Examples include:
- Carbon offsetting, and, following harm to biodiverse areas, enhancing alternative comparable biodiverse locations elsewhere (with similar endemic species or ecosystem functions).
- Mechanisms include Payment for Ecosystem Services (PES), biodiversity compensation funds into which projects must pay, biodiversity banks selling offsetting credits, and more ad hoc project-by-project solutions, all supported by national or local offsetting laws. Early biodiversity risk screening, through tools like the integrated biodiversity assessment, can help planners compile and evaluate data prior to project implementation, further mitigating harms. Offsetting is proposed as a last resort, as this suffers inherent distribution challenges (gains are felt in locations and communities not suffering the costs), while impact assessments have revealed mixed results.

[a] Such as intact frontier landscapes, biodiversity endemism hotspots, protected areas, forests liable to deforestation, landscapes with topographical or earthquake hazards, and other vulnerable landscapes.
[b] The Business and Biodiversity Offsets Program (BBOP) is one such program.

**Box 4.3:** The World Bank Environment and Social Framework

The Environmental and Social Standards set out the requirements for borrowers relating to the identification and assessment of environmental and social risks and impacts associated with projects supported by the Bank through Investment Project Financing. The Bank believes that the application of these standards, by focusing on the identification and management of environmental and social risks, will support borrowers in their goal to reduce poverty and increase prosperity in a sustainable manner for the benefit of the environment and their citizens. The standards will: (a) support borrowers in achieving good international practice relating to environmental and social sustainability; (b) assist borrowers in fulfilling their national and international environmental and social obligations; (c) enhance nondiscrimination, transparency, participation, accountability, and governance; and (d) enhance the sustainable development outcomes of projects through ongoing stakeholder engagement.

The 10 Environmental and Social Standards establish the standards that the borrower and the project will meet through the project life cycle, as follows:

- Environmental and Social Standard 1: Assessment and Management of Environmental and Social Risks and Impacts.
- Environmental and Social Standard 2: Labor and Working Conditions.
- Environmental and Social Standard 3: Resource Efficiency and Pollution Prevention and Management.
- Environmental and Social Standard 4: Community Health and Safety.
- Environmental and Social Standard 5: Land Acquisition, Restrictions on Land Use and Involuntary Resettlement.
- Environmental and Social Standard 6: Biodiversity Conservation and Sustainable Management of Living Natural Resources.
- Environmental and Social Standard 7: Indigenous Peoples/Sub-Saharan African Historically Underserved Traditional Local Communities.
- Environmental and Social Standard 8: Cultural Heritage.
- Environmental and Social Standard 9: Financial Intermediaries.
- Environmental and Social Standard 10: Stakeholder Engagement and Information Disclosure.

Environmental and Social Standard 1 applies to all projects for which Bank Investment Project Financing is sought. ESS1 establishes the importance of: (a) the Borrower's existing environmental and social framework in addressing the risks and impacts of the project; (b) an integrated environmental and social assessment to identify the risks and impacts of a project; (c) effective community engagement through disclosure of project-related information, consultation and effective feedback; and (d) management of environmental and social risks and impacts by the Borrower throughout the project life cycle. The Bank requires that all environmental and social risks and impacts of the project be addressed as part of the environmental and social assessment conducted in accordance with ESS1. ESS2–10 set out the obligations of the borrower in identifying and addressing environmental and social risks and impacts that may require particular attention. These standards establish objectives and requirements to avoid, minimize, reduce, and mitigate risks and impacts, and where significant residual impacts remain, to compensate for or offset such impacts.

*Source:* Based on the World Bank Environmental and Social Framework (World Bank 2017b).

## Social risks associated with transport sector operations

Social risks are closely linked with environmental risks, as both communities and their environments are affected by transport projects, both directly and indirectly. In addition to the strategic environmental and social assessments recommended above, BRI projects should consider social risks related to the completion of civil works. Most broadly, social impacts need to consider all of the following:

- Direct or indirect threats to human security.

- Risks that project impacts fall disproportionately on vulnerable people(s).

- Discrimination toward individuals or groups in providing access to development resources and project benefits.

- Negative economic and social impacts relating to the involuntary taking of land or restrictions on land use.

- Risks or impacts associated with land and natural resource tenure and use.

- Impacts on the health, safety, and well-being of workers and project-affected communities.

- Risks to cultural heritage.

While all BRI projects will likely need to address some of these social impacts, the BRI poses a unique challenge to the movement of people and labor. Many transport investment projects involve construction of civil works for which the required labor force and associated goods and services cannot be fully supplied locally. In such contexts, part of the entire labor force needs to be brought in from outside. In many cases, this influx is compounded by an influx of other people ("followers") who follow the incoming workforce with the aim of selling them goods and services, or in pursuit of job or business opportunities. This rapid migration, called labor influx, can negatively affect project areas' public infrastructure, utilities, housing, sustainable resource management, and social dynamics (World Bank 2016a). A labor influx is temporary and transient, and typically occurs during or just prior to construction of a project. Management teams, governments, and local service providers are often left with insufficient time or resources to adapt and respond.

Such an influx of workers and followers can lead to adverse social and environmental impacts on local communities, especially if the communities are rural, remote, or small. Such adverse impacts may include increased demand and competition for local goods and services, which can lead to price hikes and crowding out of local consumers, increased demands on the ecosystem and natural resources, social conflicts within and between communities, increased risk of spread of communicable diseases, and increased rates of illicit behavior and crime (World Bank 2016a). Such adverse impacts are usually amplified when civil works are carried out in, or near, vulnerable communities and in other high-risk situations.

A specific concern is the propagation of sexually transmissible diseases, facilitated by both labor influx and the mobility of workers in the transport sector. Short-term migration of workers away from homes and families increases opportunities for sexual relationships with multiple partners, transforming transport routes into critical links in the propagation of HIV/AIDS (World Bank 2004). While the majority of people living with HIV are not located in Belt and Road corridor economies, new infections are on the rise in several of them. Eastern Europe and Central Asia is the only world region where the HIV epidemic continues to grow rapidly, with a 30 percent increase in annual HIV infections between 2010 and 2017 (UNAIDS 2018). The majority of people living with HIV live in Russia,[10] where new infections are on the rise, followed by Ukraine; while outside of Russia, the rate of new HIV infections is stable. In the Asia Pacific region, China, India, and Indonesia account for almost three-quarters of the total number of people living with HIV. Although new infections declined by 14 percent between 2010 and 2017, progress has slowed in recent years, and new infections are on the rise in some countries, particularly in Pakistan and the Philippines (UNAIDS 2018).

### Mitigating the risks of labor influx: World Bank best practice measures

Adequate frameworks to accompany transport investments and complementary policies in targeted countries are necessary to address such risks. Following the negative impacts of a labor influx road project supported by the World Bank in Uganda, a detailed report was prepared describing the issues and the Bank's response at corporate and project levels (World Bank 2016b). Three major lessons stand out from the experience in this report. First, it is necessary to create a clear institutional architecture and to understand and address capacity constraints. The roles and responsibilities of different parties should be clearly defined and need to be legally and contractually binding. Second, it is important to initially invest to understand the environment where the project will be implemented to identify the broad risks to poor rural communities, among others, caused by labor influx. Third, it is important to prepare and launch measures to address emerging gender risks. To include these dimensions during project preparation, the World Bank has a framework for screening investments to identify the risk profile for labor influx and determine the necessary mitigation measures (World Bank 2016a).

To mitigate risks from labor influx in Bank's projects, a comprehensive list of best practice measures was developed (World Bank 2016a; ADB et al. 2018). On the definition of roles and responsibilities, the World Bank recommends ensuring that the borrower is committed to addressing these issues; to deal with child protection risks before the project begins and throughout the project cycle; to incorporate social and environmental mitigation measures in the civil works contracts; to incorporate strong environmental and social oversight responsibilities and staffing needs in the supervising engineer's contract; and to implement a workers' code of conduct that is included in their contracts and is enforced.

---

[10] Of all people living with HIV in Eastern Europe and Central Asia, 70 percent are in Russia.

To address the risks in the communities, the World Bank suggests ensuring that local authorities be actively engaged; ensuring that adequate community-engagement and grievance-management committees be created to receive, channel, and refer or respond to complaints or issues; agreeing on identification and reporting protocols for gender-based violence and violence against children; and launching awareness campaigns for workers and communities. To reduce the risks, best-practice measures are to encourage the local recruitment of workers; to empower women and girls with job opportunities through affirmative action measures during recruitment; and to ensure that sufficient background checks are made on the workers.

Finally, to create credible institutions, it is best practice to ensure that those in power do not retaliate against people who identify risks; to collaborate with police authorities to ensure that workers' criminal behavior is punished and thus such future behavior is deterred; and to ensure that response measures are created, including a minimum package for survivors of gender-based violence.

Complementary policies are also necessary in corridor economies to limit the propagation of sexually transmissible diseases. Mobile populations along corridors, such as truck drivers, mariners, and migrant workers, are among the highly vulnerable groups. In addition, trafficking drugs, and women trafficking, and children for prostitution is of particular concern when borders open. For example, in Central Asian countries, proximity and border opening with Afghanistan was shown as a reason for increased drug use in the 2000s (Godinho et al. 2005). In that context, the World Bank recommended immediate actions for regional governments through improving surveillance, adopting and implementing targeted strategies, and scaling up work with highly vulnerable and vulnerable groups. Complementary measures to limit the risks and raise awareness of the propagation of sexually transmissible diseases along transport corridors are necessary to accompany new transport investments projects in the region.

# CHAPTER 5

## Shaping the Belt and Road Initiative: Policies and institutions

BRI investments offer opportunities for countries to improve their infrastructure, to increase trade and connectivity among themselves and the wider world, and thus to increase growth and reduce poverty. Realizing these gains will require significant complementary actions on the parts of all participants in the BRI. It will also require coming to terms with the substantial risks that large projects entail, such as the fiscal and debt-related risks. Current policy reforms require a faster pace for reality to match the ambitions of the Belt and Road Initiative.

Reforms and actions to shape future developments under the Belt and Road Initiative should be based on three core principles for Belt and Road corridor economies, including China:

- The first is transparency, including providing more information on projects more broadly. Transparency in project planning, fiscal costs and budgeting, and in procurement will improve both the effectiveness of individual infrastructure investments and national development strategies. Moreover, greater transparency is essential to build public trust in investment decisions and to encourage community involvement.

- The second is country-specific reform. Many countries have trade policies and border management practices that inhibit cross-border trade. Making it easier to import and export goods is essential for countries to reap the full benefits of BRI investments. All corridor economies would benefit from open procurement processes, stronger governance, and fiscal and debt sustainability frameworks that allow them to fully account for the potential costs of debt-financed infrastructure. Given the risks associated with BRI corridors, countries can also invest in complementary adjustment policies, social and environmental safety nets, investments in skills and other infrastructure, and mobile labor.

- The third is multilateral cooperation, including coordination across BRI projects. For countries to fully benefit from the positive spillovers of economic corridor development, they will need to work together to improve trade facilitation and border management, unify standards in building infrastructure, agree on legal standards and investor protections that will encourage further investment along BRI corridors, and manage environmental risks. It will also require finding a multilateral approach to deal with potential debt distress problems associated with the BRI and with possible investment disputes and procurement issues. In some cases, cooperation will entail deeper engagement in existing institutions, such as the WTO's Government Procurement Agreements, or regional organizations. In others, new mechanisms and institutions still need to be thought out.

Proper sequencing of reforms will be key. Some actions are urgent and need to be taken while infrastructure projects are still at the early planning stages, including ensuring the soundness of project selection and planning. Effective management of fiscal, governance, environmental, and social risks requires upfront interventions to improve debt sustainability frameworks, openness in public procurement, mechanisms to mitigate corruption opportunities, and ensure high environmental and social standards. The package of initiatives announced during the 2nd Belt and Road Forum in Beijing in April 2019 is a step in the right direction, though more work lies ahead (box 5.1). Improved transparency and data on projects are an indispensable precondition for many of these actions. This will require coordination among different actors within China-government bodies, lending institutions, private sector firms, and SOEs. A first immediate objective should be to set up a comprehensive database of BRI projects.

Other policy reforms can be implemented over time, as they aim to complement BRI investment and to deal with the consequences of the new infrastructure such as their distributional and spatial effects. For this set of actions, prioritization is also important. Border delays and restrictions to trade and FDI create large distortions that are difficult to justify in an effort aimed at improving connectivity. They also prevent countries from reaping the full benefits of BRI projects, in some cases leading to welfare losses. As the analysis shows, reducing these distortions would have large immediate payoffs. Other important reforms that aim to deepen trade agreements, support private sector participation, strengthen the legal protection of investment, and ensure that the gains from BRI are largely shared should advance as the initiative takes shape.

Shaping the Belt and Road as a truly multilateral initiative would require moving beyond bilateral arrangements. The current bilateral relationships that China has cultivated and established may be appropriate in the short term, especially during the development phases of some corridors. But developing an overarching framework for the Belt and Road Initiative would help ensure a clear path for reform going forward. Long-term institutional governance arrangements could serve several roles, including institutionalizing coordination mechanisms, providing a platform for public information and transparency, and improving standards.

### *Policy matrix of BRI reform actions*

While country circumstances differ, the following policy and practice recommendations can help countries identify the reforms needed to reap the benefits and mitigate the risks from BRI investments. Certain actions are well established practices that may only require implementation, while others may require legislation, multilateral cooperation, and expert analysis. All recommendations are only sketched in the table, and each would require a detailed action plan. The previous chapters, and especially the background papers, provide more information.

**Box 5.1:** Key initiatives launched at the 2nd Belt and Road Forum

China hosted the 2nd bi-annual BRF for International Cooperation on April 25–27, 2019. The 1st BRF was held on May 14–15, 2017. The main theme of the 2nd BRF was high-quality development of the BRI, espousing quality infrastructure and connectivity, clean, inclusive, and green BRI. President Xi Jinping in his opening speech at the Forum stressed the importance of high standards in China's BRI projects to ensure that they are of high quality, beneficial to people and sustainable. To that effect, several major initiatives were launched at the Forum, including:

**Open and Clean BRI**—the "Beijing Initiative for the Clean Silk Road" calls for international cooperation to promote transparency and integrity, and combat corruption. The initiative stresses implementation of the BRI in accordance with the spirits of the UN Convention Against Corruption and other international rules and legal frameworks; enhancing openness and transparency of government information; preventing and resolving trade and investment disputes; promoting cooperation on finance, taxation, intellectual property, and environmental protection; closely supervising BRI projects, including strict use of relevant laws and regulations in public procurement; improving awareness and capacity of participating countries and their development partners; and promoting treaties for bilateral extradition and mutual legal assistance based on relevant international conventions and treaties. These are important principles consistent with good international practices. Their successful implementation requires further operationalization through public procurement laws, policies, and guidelines, credible dispute resolution systems, and third-party monitoring and enforcement.

**Green BRI**—the "Green Investment Principles (GIPs) for the Belt and Road" call for promoting environmental friendliness, climate resilience, and social inclusiveness under new BRI investment projects. These principles are aligned with the goals of the United Nations 2030 Agenda for Sustainable Development and the Paris Agreement. They reflect international good practices in green, inclusive and sustainable development, including understanding environmental, social and governance risks; embedding sustainability into corporate governance; disclosing environmental information; adopting green supply chain management; and utilizing green financial instruments. Capacity building through collective action and enhancing communication with stakeholders are also principles to be promoted. China and other BRI participating countries would benefit from further operationalizing these good international principles by harmonizing and aligning their environmental and social standards with good international practices and by taking the network or corridor nature of the BRI into consideration while assessing environmental and social risks and mitigation options.

**Sustainable BRI**—China's ministry of finance launched a Debt Sustainability Framework (DSF) for participating countries of the BRI to promote their sustainable economic and social development while ensuring debt sustainability. The proposed DSF builds on the IMF/World Bank DSF for Low Income Countries. As discussed in chapter 4, while the launching of the BRI DSF is a step in the right direction, its effectiveness depends on whether and how participating countries and financial institutions use it. Currently, using the BRI DSF is voluntary. Moreover, the credibility of the BRI DSF will depend on its users' ability to collect relevant data, share such data with those involved, and make the findings of the debt sustainability analysis public.

**Multilateral Infrastructure and Connectivity Investments**—China's ministry of finance and a number of multilateral development institutions signed a memorandum of understanding to establish a multilateral cooperation platform - the Multilateral Cooperation Center for Development Finance. The signatories are currently working together to establish the Center, which is expected to mobilize resources to support information sharing, capacity building, and project preparation activities. This is an important initiative to support the broader development of high-quality infrastructure and connectivity investments following good international practices and making use of the multilateral development institutions' experience.

**Table 5.1:** BRI reform actions

| What to do? | By whom? | | | When? | | |
|---|---|---|---|---|---|---|
| | China | Belt and Road corridor economies | Cooperatively | Upfront | Short-term | Medium-term |
| **Complementary reforms** | | | | | | |
| *Integration and corridor development* | | | | | | |
| Promote trade facilitation reform to reduce bottlenecks through, among others, risk-based approaches to border management, modern information, and communications technology systems with reengineered and streamlined practices. | ✓ | ✓ | ✓ | | ✓ | |
| Reduce trade policy barriers, including those in service sectors such as transport, and move toward deepening trade agreements that would support BRI investment (including policy areas such as investment, competition, visa and asylum, and public procurement). | ✓ | ✓ | ✓ | | ✓ | |
| Ensure the soundness of project selection and planning. For example, require a full description of the expected benefits from the project, including further economic activity likely to be created by the investment, and the direct and indirect effects. Consider complementary investment, including in information and communications technology. | ✓ | ✓ | ✓ | ✓ | | |
| Achieve interoperability of transport infrastructure through harmonized laws, common institutional frameworks, and norms, standards, and practices based on internationally agreed standards. | ✓ | ✓ | ✓ | | ✓ | |
| *Private sector participation* | | | | | | |
| Strengthen legal protection of investment through rules and their enforcement. Establish cooperative and neutral mechanisms for dispute settlement and dispute prevention. | ✓ | ✓ | ✓ | | | ✓ |
| Design public investment to avoid crowding out the private sector from commercially viable ventures. Prioritize projects whose structuring in the short to medium term is not fully commercial or not commercial at all, but that have a high developmental impact. | ✓ | ✓ | | ✓ | | |
| Support the reform of the regulatory environment at the national level and through policy experimentation and careful planning of special economic zones (SEZs). For example, fully exploit the synergy between SEZs and connectivity infrastructure. | ✓ | ✓ | | | | ✓ |
| *Inclusiveness* | | | | | | |
| Ensure an adequate policy framework to deal with the adjustment costs imposed by trade shocks from competition with trading partners, including social security and labor policies (such as education and training). | ✓ | ✓ | | | | ✓ |

Table 5.1: BRI reform actions (cont.)

| What to do? | By whom? | | | When? | | |
|---|---|---|---|---|---|---|
| | China | Belt and Road corridor economies | Cooperatively | Upfront | Short-term | Medium-term |
| Address potentially negative effects of territorial inequality by reducing direct constraints to internal labor mobility and indirect constraints associated with distortions in land and housing markets. Improve the attractiveness of peripheral areas through complementary investment in logistics, transport, and skill development. | ✓ | ✓ | | | | ✓ |
| Ensure that cities and subnational hubs can benefit from BRI projects by investing in logistics to foster local hubs, improving urban transport and other services where population influx is expected, and investing in human capital to service existing and new investment flows. | ✓ | ✓ | | | | ✓ |
| **Managing risks** | | | | | | |
| *Fiscal risks* | | | | | | |
| Publicly disclose the terms and conditions of BRI projects, including loan-by-loan information on public loans. Coordinate different actors within China—government bodies, lending institutions, private sector firms, and SOEs. Set up a comprehensive database of BRI projects. | ✓ | | | ✓ | | |
| China's lending institutions can verify that their lending operations (toward a foreign government, public entity of a foreign government or with a guarantee of a foreign government) are in adherence with a borrowing country's primary and secondary legislation and that the amount of financing appropriately reflects the value of the project. | ✓ | | | ✓ | | |
| Systematically use debt sustainability analysis prepared under the BRI DSF to guide borrowing volumes and terms with a view of safeguarding debt sustainability informed by WB-IMF DSAs. Offer publicly available templates for financing arrangements under the BRI and refrain from using confidentiality clauses. | ✓ | | | ✓ | | |
| Make participation in debt restructuring public. Have a debt restructuring framework in place that is conducive to providing required relief in a timely fashion, and enables China to participate in a collaborative approach with other creditors, when appropriate. | ✓ | | | ✓ | | |
| Strengthen the publication of comprehensive public debt reports, covering general government debt, government guarantees, and the debt of non-financial public enterprises. | | ✓ | | ✓ | | |
| Establish comprehensive fiscal frameworks with proper reporting of government operations, adequate monitoring and management of fiscal risks, multiyear budgets, and transparent procurement practices. | | ✓ | | ✓ | | |

**Table 5.1:** BRI reform actions (cont.)

| What to do? | By whom? | | | When? | | |
|---|---|---|---|---|---|---|
| | China | Belt and Road corridor economies | Cooperatively | Upfront | Short-term | Medium-term |
| Refrain from taking on collateralized loans that breach applicable Negative Pledge Clauses and that are collateralized through unrelated asset or revenue streams and ensure that reduced risks arising from collateralization are reflected in improved financial terms. | | ✓ | | ✓ | | |
| Improve regulatory frameworks for public-private partnership and procurement processes. | ✓ | ✓ | ✓ | ✓ | | |
| **Governance risks** | | | | | | |
| Move toward internationally accepted good practices in BRI project procurement. At a minimum, ensure that projects above a threshold are awarded through open national competition among Chinese companies, including foreign-invested enterprises (as agreed in the 2005 Paris Declaration on Aid Effectiveness). | ✓ | | | ✓ | | |
| Apply national procurement laws to BRI procurement to increase the transparency and competitiveness of BRI project procurement. | | ✓ | | ✓ | | |
| Make greater use of trade agreements, including the WTO Government Procurement Agreement, to increase the likelihood of applying good procurement practices. | ✓ | ✓ | ✓ | ✓ | | |
| Increase transparency by enhancing disclosure of data and documents at all stages of the contracting process. | | ✓ | | ✓ | | |
| Make use of both supply-side interventions (construction sector transparency, red flags, integrity pacts) and demand-side mechanisms (community monitoring) to addresses problems of monitoring, reporting, and enforcing anti-corruption. | ✓ | ✓ | | ✓ | | |
| **Environmental and social risks** | | | | | | |
| Conduct strategic social and environment assessment at the corridor level, in addition to standard assessments at the project level. Move toward internationally accepted good practices to address environmental risks. (The World Bank's Environmental and Social Framework provides 10 standards and a comprehensive treatment of "best practices.") | ✓ | ✓ | ✓ | ✓ | | |
| Move toward internationally accepted good practices to address social risks due to land acquisition and resettlement; risks to indigenous peoples; risks from work camps with a large influx of outsiders; and risks to community health and safety around construction sites. | ✓ | ✓ | ✓ | ✓ | | |

*Note:* Depending on the policy action, cooperation may be among all Belt and Road corridor economies (including China) or among subsets of economies (such as countries along a specific transport corridor, neighboring countries, or countries belonging to an existing regional organization).

# REFERENCES

ADB (Asian Development Bank). 2007. "Improving Local Governance and Service Delivery: Citizen Report Card Learning Tool Kit." Mandaluyong City, Philippines: ADB. Available at: http://www.citizenreportcard.com/crccom/crc/pdf/manual.pdf.

————. 2017. *Meeting Asia's Infrastructure Needs.* Mandaluyong City, Philippines: ADB.

ADB, UKAID, JICA (Japan International Cooperation Agency), and World Bank. 2018. The WEB of Transport Corridors in South Asia. Washington, DC: World Bank.

Alexeeva, V., C. Queiroz, and S. Ishihara. 2008. "Monitoring Road Works Contracts and Unit Costs for Enhanced Governance in Sub-Saharan Africa." Transport Paper 21, World Bank, Washington, DC.

Arvis, J.-F., V. Vesin, R. Carruthers, C. Ducruet, and P. de Langen. 2019. *Maritime Networks, Port Efficiency, and Hinterland Connectivity in the Mediterranean. International Development in Focus.* Washington, DC: World Bank.

Asher, S., T. Garg, and P. Novosad. 2017. The Ecological Footprint of Transportation Infrastructure. Working Paper. Available at: http://www.greengrowthknowledge.org/sites/default/files/downloads/resource/Asher_The%20Ecological%20Footprint%20of%20Transportation%20Infrastructure.pdf.

Bandiera, L., and V. Tsiropoulos. 2019. "A Framework to Assess Debt Sustainability and Fiscal Risks under the Belt and Road Initiative." Unpublished working paper, World Bank, Washington, DC.

Baniya, S., N. Rocha, and M. Ruta. 2018. "Trade Effects of the New Silk Road: A Gravity Analysis." Policy Research Working Paper 8694, World Bank, Washington, DC.

Bartley Johns, M., C. Kerswell, J. L. Clarke, and G. McLinden. 2018. "Trade Facilitation Challenges and Reform Priorities for Maximizing the Impact of the Belt and Road Initiative." MTI Global Practice Discussion Paper 4, World Bank, Washington, DC.

Bastos, P. 2018. "Exposure of Belt and Road Economies to China Trade Shocks." Policy Research Working Paper WPS 8503, World Bank, Washington, DC.

Benitez-Lopez, A., R. Alkemade, and P. A. Verweij. 2010. "The Impacts of Roads and Other Infrastructure on Mammal and Bird Populations: A Meta-Analysis." *Biological Conservation* 143 (6): 1307–16.

Bird, J., M. Lebrand, and A. Venables. 2019. "The Belt and Road Initiative: Reshaping Economic Geography in Central Asia?" Policy Research Working Paper WPS 8807, World Bank, Washington, DC.

Boffa, M. 2018. "Trade Linkages between the Belt and Road Economies." Policy Research Working Paper WPS 8423, World Bank, Washington, DC.

Brautigam, D., and J. Hwang. 2016. "Eastern Promises: New Data on Chinese Loans in Africa, 2000 to 2014." Working Paper 4, China–Africa Research Initiative, School of Advanced International Studies, Johns Hopkins University, Washington, DC.

Bruschi, D., D. A. Garcia, F. Gugliermetti, and F. Cumo. 2015. "Characterizing the Fragmentation Level of Italy's National Parks Due to Transportation Infrastructures." *Transportation Research Part D: Transport and Environment* 36: 18–28.

Bullock, R., Z. Liu, and H. Tan. 2019. "Belt and Road Initiative: The Land-based Freight Market Analysis." Unpublished working paper, World Bank, Washington, DC.

Cader, M., A. Cantor, S. Shao, and M. Liu. 2019. "Co-Investment and Creating Markets along the Belt and Road." Unpublished working paper, World Bank, Washington, DC.

Calderon, C., and L. Serven. 2014. "Infrastructure, Growth, and Inequality: An Overview." Policy Research Working Paper 7304, World Bank, Washington, DC.

Caliendo, L., and F. Parro. 2015. "Estimates of the Trade and Welfare Effects of NAFTA." *The Review of Economic Studies* 82 (1): 1–44.

Chen, M., and C. Lin. 2018. "Foreign Investment across the Belt and Road: Patterns, Determinants and Effects." Policy Research Working Paper 8607, World Bank, Washington, DC.

Constantinescu, C., A. Mattoo, and M. Ruta. 2018. "Trade in Developing East Asia: How It Has Changed and Why It Matters." Policy Research Working Paper 8533, World Bank, Washington, DC.

Constantinescu, C., and M. Ruta. 2018. "How Old is the Belt and Road Initiative? Long Term Patterns of Chinese Exports to BRI Economies." MTI Practice Note 6, World Bank, Washington, DC.

Deloitte. 2018. "Embracing the BRI Ecosystem in 2018: Navigating Pitfalls and Seizing Opportunities." Available at: https://www2.deloitte.com/content/dam/insights/us/articles/4406_Belt-and-road-initiative/4406_Embracing-the-BRI-ecosystem.pdf.

Deng, X., J. Huang, E. Uchida, S. Rozelle, and J. Gibson. 2011. "Pressure Cookers or Pressure Valves: Do Roads Lead to Deforestation in China?" *Journal of Environmental Economics and Management* 61 (1): 79–94.

Derudder, B., X. Lia, and C. Kunaka. 2018. "Connectivity Along Overland Corridors of the Belt and Road Initiative." MTI Global Practice Discussion Paper 6, World Bank, Washington, DC.

De Soyres, F., A. Mulabdic, and M. Ruta. 2019. "Common Transport Infrastructure: A Quantitative Model and Estimates from the Belt and Road Initiative." Policy Research Working Paper WPS 8801, World Bank, Washington, DC.

De Soyres, F., A. Mulabdic, S. Murray, N. Rocha, and M. Ruta. 2018. "How Much Will the Belt and Road Initiative Reduce Trade Costs?" Policy Research Working Paper WPS 8614, World Bank, Washington, DC.

Devadas, S., and S. M. Pennings. 2018. "Assessing the Effect of Public Capital on Growth: An Extension of the World Bank Long-Term Growth Model." Policy Research Working Paper 8604, World Bank, Washington, DC.

Djankov, S., and C. Freund. 2002. "Trade Flows in the Former Soviet Union, 1987 to 1996." *Journal of Comparative Economics* 30 (1): 76–90.

Donaldson, D. 2018. "Railroads of the Raj: Estimating the Impact of Transportation Infrastructure." American Economic Review 108 (4–5): 899–934.

Doree, A. 2004. "Collusion in the Dutch Construction Industry: An Industrial Organization Perspective." Building Research and Information 32 (2): 146–156.

Duranton, G., and A. J. Venables. 2018. "Place-based Policies for Development." Policy Research Working Paper WPS 8410, World Bank, Washington, DC.

Echandi, R. 2018. "The Debate on Treaty-Based Investor–State Dispute Settlement (ISDS): Empirical Evidence (1987–2017) and Policy Implications." *ICSID Review, Foreign Investment Law Journal* 33 (2018).

Farole, T. 2017. "Special Economic Zones and Industrialization: History, Recent Development, and Future Challenge." Unpublished working paper, World Bank, Washington, DC.

Flyvbjerg, B. 2014. "What You Should Know about Megaprojects and Why: An Overview." *Project Management Journal* 45 (2): 6–19.

———. 2017. "Introduction: The Iron Law of Megaproject Management." In The Oxford Handbook of Megaproject Management, edited by B. Flyvbjerg, 1–18. Oxford, UK: Oxford University Press.

Frankopan, P. 2017. The Silk Roads: A New History of the World. London: Bloomsbury.

Freund, C., A. Mulabdic, and M. Ruta. 2019. "Is 3D Printing a Threat to Global Trade? The Trade Effects You Didn't Hear About." Unpublished working paper, World Bank, Washington, DC.

Ghossein, T., B. Hoekman, and A. Shingal. 2018. "Public Procurement in the Belt and Road Initiative." Background paper, World Bank, Washington, DC.

Godinho, J., T. Novotny, H. Tadesse, and A. Vinokur. 2005. "HIV/AIDS and Tuberculosis in Central Asia: Country Profiles." Working Paper, World Bank, Washington, DC.

Goosem, M. 2015. "Vulnerability and Climatic Conditions: Particular Challenges for Road Planning, Construction, and Maintenance." *In Handbook of Road Ecology*, edited by R. van der Ree, D. J. Smith, and C. Grilo, 397–406. West Sussex, UK: Wiley.

Gould, D. M. 2018. "Critical Connections: Promoting Economic Growth and Resilience in Europe and Central Asia." Europe and Central Asia Studies, World Bank, Washington, DC.

Guha, P., and D. Sivaev. 2018. "Belt and the City: Complementary Policies and Investments to Enhance City Competitiveness." Unpublished working paper, World Bank, Washington, DC.

Hallward-Driemeier, M., and G. Nayyar. 2018. *Trouble in the Making? The Future of Manufacturing-Led Development.* Washington, DC: World Bank.

Head, K., and T. Mayer. 2014. "Gravity Equations: Workhorse, Toolkit, and Cookbook." Chapter 3 in *Handbook of International Economics,* edited by G. Gopinath, E. Helpman, and K. Rogoff, 131–195. Amsterdam: Elsevier.

Helsingen, H., B. Milligan, M. Dailey, and N. Bhagabati. 2018. *Greening China's Belt & Road Initiative in Myanmar. Yangon, Myanmar:* World Wildlife Fund.

Hillman, J. 2018. "How Big Is China's Belt and Road?" Blog post, Center for Strategic and International Studies, Washington, DC. Available at: https://www.csis.org/analysis/how-big-chinas-belt-and-road.

Hoare, A., L. Hong, and J. Hein. 2018. "The Role of Investors in Promoting Sustainable Infrastructure under the Belt and Road Initiative." Research Paper, Chatham House, London.

Hofmann, C., A. Osnago, and M. Ruta. 2017. "Horizontal Depth: A New Database on the Content of Preferential Trade Agreements." Policy Research Working Paper WPS 7981, World Bank, Washington, DC.

Howkins, J. 2013. "How to Note: Reducing Corruption in Infrastructure Sectors." Evidence on Demand, UK Department of International Development, London. Available at: http://www.undp-aciac.org/publications/ac/publications/EoD_Consultancy_May2013_Reducing_Corruption_in_Infrastructure.pdf.

Hummels, D., and G. Schaur. 2013. "Time as a Trade Barrier." *American Economic Review* 103 (7): 2935–59.

IMF (International Monetary Fund), World Bank, and WTO (World Trade Organization). 2017. "Making Trade and Engine of Growth for All: The Case for Trade and for Policies to Facilitate Adjustment." Policy Paper, IMF, World Bank, and WTO, Washington, DC.

Ibisch, P. L., M. T. Hoffmann, S. Kreft, G. Pe'er, V. Kati, L. Biber-Freudenberger, D. A. DellaSala, M. M. Vale, P. R. Hobson, and N. Selva. 2016. "A Global Map of Roadless Areas and Their Conservation Status." Science 354 (6318): 1423–27.

International Transport Forum. 2016. Capacity to Grow: Transport Infrastructure Needs for Future Trade Growth. Paris.

Isaksson, A.-S., and A. Kotsadamb. 2018. "Chinese Aid and Local Corruption." Journal of Public Economics 159 (2018): 146–159.

JICA (Japan International Cooperation Agency). 2008. "National Highway No. 5 Improvement Project." Vietnam–Japan Joint Evaluation Team 2007, JICA, Tokyo. Available at: https://www.jica.go.jp/english/our_work/evaluation/oda_loan/post/2008/pdf/e_project29_full.pdf.

———. 2009. "Ex Post Evaluation of Japanese ODA Loan Project: National Highway No. 5 Improvement Project (I) (II)." Report prepared by Masumi Shimamura, Mitsubishi UFJ Research and Consulting Co., Ltd. Tokyo: JICA. Available at: https://www2.jica.go.jp/en/evaluation/pdf/2009_VNV-5_4.pdf.

Jolliffe, D. M., and E. B. Prydz. 2016. "Estimating International Poverty Lines from Comparable National Thresholds." Policy Research Working Paper WPS 7606, World Bank, Washington, DC.

Kaczan, D. J. 2016. "Can Roads Contribute to Forest Transitions?" PhD Thesis, Sanford School of Public Policy and Nicholas School of the Environment, Duke University, Durham, NC.

Kelly, T. 2018. "The Digital Silk Road: Development opportunities within the Belt and Road Initiative." Unpublished working paper, World Bank, Washington, DC.

Kenny, C. 2006. "Measuring and Reducing the Impact of Corruption in Infrastructure." Policy Research Working Paper 4099, World Bank, Washington, DC.

Kher, P., and T. Tran. 2018. "Investment Protection along the Belt & Road." MTI Global Practice Discussion Paper 12, World Bank, Washington, DC.

Kunaka, C. 2018. "Institutional Arrangements for Band and Road Corridors." Unpublished working paper, World Bank, Washington, DC.

Laird, J., and A. J. Venables. 2017. "Transport Investment and Economic Performance: A Framework for Project Appraisal." *Transport Policy* 56 (May): 1–11.

Lall, S. V., and M. Lebrand. 2019. "Who Wins, Who Loses? Understanding the Spatially Differentiated Effects of Belt and Road Initiative." Policy Research Working Paper WPS 8806, World Bank, Washington, DC.

Lebrand, M., and C. Briceño-Garmendia. 2018. "Transport Connectivity in Europe, Central Asia and China: Assessing the Needs and Effects of BRI Interventions."

Leigland, J. 2018. "Public–Private Partnerships in Developing Countries: The Emerging Evidence-based Critique." *The World Bank Research Observer* 33 (1): 103–134.

Li, Xin, Yingling Fan, and Lan Wu. 2017. "CO2 emissions and Expansion of Railway, Road, Airline and Inland Waterway Networks over the 1985–2013 Period in China: A Time Series Analysis." *Transportation Research Part D: Transport and Environment* 57 (September): 130–40. http://dx.doi.org/10.1016/j.trd.2017.09.008.

Linn, J. F., and L. Zucker, 2019. "An 'Inside-out' Perspective on the Impact of the Belt and Road Initiative in Central Asia and the South Caucasus: How to Maximize its Benefits and Manage its Risks. Emerging Markets Forum." Forthcoming, Oxford University Press.

Losos, E., A. Pfaff, L. Olander, S. Mason, and S. Morgan. 2018. "Reducing Environmental Risks from Belt and Road Initiative Investments in Transportation Infrastructure." Policy Research Working Paper 8718, World Bank, Washington, DC.

Maliszewska, M., and D. van der Mensbrugghe. 2019. "The Belt and Road Initiative: Macro and Sectoral Impacts." Policy Research Working Paper WPS 8814, World Bank, Washington, DC.

Millward, J. 2013. The Silk Road: *A Very Short Introduction*. Oxford, UK: Oxford University Press.

Notteboom, T. 2017. "PortGraphic: Top 15 Container Ports in Europe in 2016—Has TEU Growth Resumed?" PortEconomics. Available at: http://www.porteconomics.eu/2017/03/26/portgraphic-top-15-container-ports-in-europe-in-2016-has-teu-growth-resumed/.

OECD (Organisation for Economic Co-operation and Development). 2015. *State-Owned Enterprises in the Development Process*. Paris: OECD Publishing. https://read.oecd-ilibrary.org/finance-and-investment/state-owned-enterprises-in-the-development-process_9789264229617-en#page8.

Rastogi, C., and J. F. Arvis. 2014. *The Eurasian Connection: Supply-Chain Efficiency along the Modern Silk Route through Central Asia*. Washington, DC: World Bank.

Ravallion, M., and S. Chen. 2011. "Weakly Relative Poverty." *Review of Economics and Statistics* 93 (4): 1251–1261.

Reed, T., and A. Trubetskoy. 2019. "Assessing the Value of Market Access from Belt and Road Projects." Policy Research Working Paper WPS 8815, World Bank, Washington, DC.

Rozenberg, J., and M. Fay. 2019. *Beyond the Gap: How Countries Can Afford the Infrastructure They Need while Protecting the Planet.* Washington, DC: World Bank.

Sieber, N. 2014. "Road Corruption Unmasked." BalkanInsight. Available at: http://www.balkaninsight.com/en/article/road-corruption-unmasked-1.

Taglioni, D., and D. Z. Gurara. 2018. "Private Sector Participation in the Belt and Road Initiative." Draft paper, IFC and IMF, Washington, DC.

UNAIDS (Joint United Nations Program on HIV/AIDS). 2018. *Global AIDS Update 2018: Miles to Go: Closing Gaps, Breaking Barriers, Righting Injustices. Geneva:* UNAIDS. Available at: http://www.unaids.org/sites/default/files/media_asset/miles-to-go_en.pdf.

We Are Social. 2018. *Global Digital Report 2018.* New York: We Are Social. Available at: https://digitalreport.wearesocial.com/.

Wiederer, C. 2018. "Logistics Infrastructure along the Belt and Road Initiative Economies." MTI Practice Notes 5, World Bank, Washington, DC.

World Bank. 2004. "Taming HIV/AIDS on Africa's Roads." Findings Note 236, World Bank, Washington, DC.

———. 2007. T*he Many Faces of Corruption: Tracking Vulnerabilities at Sector Level.* Washington, DC: World Bank.

———. 2009. World Development Report 2009: *Reshaping Economic Geography.* Washington, DC: World Bank.

———. 2016a. "Managing the Risks of Adverse Impacts on Communities from Temporary Project Induced Labor Influx." Guidance Note, World Bank, Washington, DC. Available at: http://pubdocs.worldbank.org/en/497851495202591233/Managing-Risk-of-Adverse-impact-from-project-labor-influx.pdf.

———. 2016b. "Uganda Transport Sector Development Project—Additional Financing: Lessons Learned and Agenda for Action." World Bank, Washington, DC. Available at: http://documents.worldbank.org/curated/en/948341479845064519/pdf/110455-BR-PUBLIC-LESSONS-LEARNT-IDA-SecM2016-0204.pdf.

———. 2016c. *World Development Report 2016: Digital Dividends.* Washington, DC: World Bank.

———. 2017a. Public–Private Partnerships Reference Guide, Version 3. Washington, DC: World Bank. Available at: https://openknowledge.worldbank.org/handle/10986/29052.

———. 2017b *The World Bank Environmental and Social Framework.* World Bank, Washington DC

———. 2018a. A Glass Half Full : The Promise of Regional Trade in South Asia. Washington, DC: World Bank. Available at: https://openknowledge.worldbank.org/handle/10986/30246.

———. 2018b. "Indicative TEN-T Investment Action Plan." Washington, DC: World Bank. Available at: https://ec.europa.eu/neighbourhood-enlargement/sites/near/files/ten-t_iap_web-dec13.pdf.

———. 2018c. "2018 Private Participation in Infrastructure (PPI) Annual Report." Washington, DC: World Bank. Availlable at: https://ppi.worldbank.org/~/media/GIAWB/PPI/Documents/Global-Notes/PPI_2018_AnnualReport

———. 2018d. "Procuring Infrastructure PPPs." Washington, DC: World Bank. Available at: http://bpp.worldbank.org/

World Economic Forum. 2018. *Global Competitiveness Report.* Cologny, Switzerland: World Economic Forum.

World Justice Project. 2018. "Our Work." Washington, DC and Seattle, WA: World Justice Project. Available at: https://worldjusticeproject.org/our-work/wjp-rule-law-index.

Zhang, C., and J. Gutman. 2015. "Aid Procurement and the Development of Local Industry: A Question for Africa." Global Economy and Development Working Paper 88, Brookings Institution, Washington, DC.

# APPENDIXES

## *Appendix A. Economies covered by this report*

| | Economy | WBG region | | Economy | WBG region |
|---|---|---|---|---|---|
| 1 | Kenya | AFR | 37 | Poland | ECA |
| 2 | Tanzania | AFR | 38 | Romania | ECA |
| 3 | Brunei Darussalam | EAP | 39 | Russian Federation | ECA |
| 4 | Cambodia | EAP | 40 | Serbia | ECA |
| 5 | China | EAP | 41 | Slovak Republic | ECA |
| 6 | Hong Kong SAR, China | EAP | 42 | Slovenia | ECA |
| 7 | Indonesia | EAP | 43 | Tajikistan | ECA |
| 8 | Lao PDR | EAP | 44 | Turkey | ECA |
| 9 | Malaysia | EAP | 45 | Turkmenistan | ECA |
| 10 | Mongolia | EAP | 46 | Ukraine | ECA |
| 11 | Myanmar | EAP | 47 | Uzbekistan | ECA |
| 12 | Philippines | EAP | 48 | Bahrain | MENA |
| 13 | Singapore | EAP | 49 | Djibouti | MENA |
| 14 | Taiwan, China | EAP | 50 | Egypt, Arab Rep. | MENA |
| 15 | Thailand | EAP | 51 | Iran, Islamic Rep. | MENA |
| 16 | Timor-Leste | EAP | 52 | Iraq | MENA |
| 17 | Vietnam | EAP | 53 | Israel | MENA |
| 18 | Albania | ECA | 54 | Jordan | MENA |
| 19 | Armenia | ECA | 55 | Kuwait | MENA |
| 20 | Azerbaijan | ECA | 56 | Lebanon | MENA |
| 21 | Belarus | ECA | 57 | Oman | MENA |
| 22 | Bosnia and Herzegovina | ECA | 58 | Qatar | MENA |
| 23 | Bulgaria | ECA | 59 | Saudi Arabia | MENA |
| 24 | Croatia | ECA | 60 | Syrian Arab Republic | MENA |
| 25 | Czech Republic | ECA | 61 | United Arab Emirates | MENA |
| 26 | Estonia | ECA | 62 | West Bank and Gaza | MENA |
| 27 | Georgia | ECA | 63 | Yemen, Rep. | MENA |
| 28 | Greece | ECA | 64 | Afghanistan | SAR |
| 29 | Hungary | ECA | 65 | Bangladesh | SAR |
| 30 | Kazakhstan | ECA | 66 | Bhutan | SAR |
| 31 | Kyrgyz Republic | ECA | 67 | India | SAR |
| 32 | Latvia | ECA | 68 | Maldives | SAR |
| 33 | Lithuania | ECA | 69 | Nepal | SAR |
| 34 | Moldova | ECA | 70 | Pakistan | SAR |
| 35 | Montenegro | ECA | 71 | Sri Lanka | SAR |
| 36 | North Macedonia | ECA | | | |

*Note:* AFR = Sub-Saharan Africa; EAP = East Asia and the Pacific; ECA = Europe and Central Asia; MENA = the Middle East and North Africa; SAR = South Asia.

## Appendix B. BRI road, rail, and port investments

### Table B1 : Silk Road Economic Belt ("Belt")

| Corridor | Nº | Project | Improved Segment | Countries | Improvement type | Status | Details | Status Date |
|---|---|---|---|---|---|---|---|---|
| CHINA–MONGOLIA–RUSSIA ECONOMIC CORRIDOR (CMREC) | 1. | Central Rail Corridor | Ulan-Ude–Ulaanbaatar–Erenhot | Russia Mongolia | Rail upgrade | Operational | 30-Sep-18 | |
| | | | Erenhot–Beijing–Tianjin | China | Rail upgrade | | | |
| | 2. | Northern Rail Corridor | Kuragino–Kyzyl | Russia | New rail | Planning | Construction started on section to Ovoot coal mine, to finish in 2019. Section beyond Ovoot is only planned. Final feasibility study approved in April 2018. | 10-Apr-18 |
| | | | Kyzyl–Arts | Russia | New rail | | | |
| | | | Suur–Ovoot | Mongolia | | | | |
| | | | Ovoot–Erdenet | Mongolia | New rail | | | |
| | | | Erdenet–Salkhit | Mongolia | Rail reconstruction | | | |
| | 3. | Western Rail Corridor | Arts Suur–Urumqi | Mongolia, China | New rail | Proposed | Proposed under Mongolia national rail policy and joint China–Mongolia–Russsia declaration. | 25-Nov-18 |
| | 4. | Eastern Rail Corridor | Choibalsan–Bichigt | Mongolia | New rail | Proposed | Proposed and still being discussed. China, Russia, and Mongolia ready to operationalize the agreement. | 23-Jan-18 |
| | | | Bichigt–Chifeng | China | New rail | | | |
| | | | Chifeng–Jinzhou | China | Rail reconstruction | | | |
| | 5. | Nizhneleninskoye Bridge | Leninskoye–Tongjiang | China, Russia | New rail | Under construction | China's side of the railway bridge has been completed already. Massive floods delayed work on the Russia side. the Russia to complete its section in 2018. | 13-Nov-18 |
| | 6. | Seaside 1 Corridor (Primorye-1) | Pogranichny crossing | China, Russia | Border cost reduction | Operational | | 26-Sep-18 |
| | | | Poltavka crossing | China, Russia | Border cost reduction | | | |
| | | | Harbin–Ussuriysk | China, Russia | Rail upgrade | | | |
| | | | Ussuriysk–China border | Russia | Road reconstruction | | | |
| | | | Vladivostok–Nakhodka | Russia | New divided road | | | |
| | | | Vostochny Port | Russia | New seaport | | | |
| | 7. | Seaside 2 Corridor (Primorye-2) | Choibalsan–Arixan | Mongolia | New rail | Operational | Launched this year. The first test overload occurred in April 2018 and in September, a new Hunchun–Zarubino–Ningbo transit line was opened within the Primorye-2. The corridor connects Hunchun, a border city in Jilin Province, and the port of Zarubino. | 13-Nov-18 |
| | | | Kraskino-Hunchun crossing | China, Russia | Border cost reduction | | | |
| | | | China border–Zarubino | Russia | New rail | | | |
| | | | China border–Zarubino | Russia | New divided road | | | |
| | | Zarubino Port | Russia | New seaport | | | | |
| | 8. | Highway AH-3 | Ulan-Ude–Erenhot | Russia, Mongolia | New road | Operational | The link was tested for operations in August 2016 and has been in use since. | 30-Sep-18 |
| | | | Erehnot–Jining | China | Road upgrade | | | |
| | 9. | Highway AH-4 | Novosibirsk–Khovd–Urumqi | Russia, Mongolia, China | New road | Operational | Open for use but construction still ongoing. Part of Asian Highway 4 which runs from Novosibirsk to Karachi. | 30-Sep-18 |
| NEW EURASIAN LAND BRIDGE | 10. | Southern Coal Railway | Khuut–Tavan Tolgoi–Gushun Suhait | Mongolia | New rail | Under construction | Civil works underway in Mongolia, scheduled completion in 2019. Chinese section operational. | 12-Feb-18 |
| | | | Gushun Suhait–Baotou | China | New rail | | | |
| | 11. | Khorgos–Aktau Railway | Khorgos–Zhetygen | Kazakhstan | New hicap rail | Under construction | The rail links what will soon be the world's biggest dry port Khorgos (China) and Aktau port (Kazakhstan). When fully operational, the railway will enable transportation of cargo along the Caspian Sea and the Caucasus to Europe, and through the Islamic Republic of Iran to the Persian Gulf. | 15-Apr-17 |
| | | | Jezkazgan–Saksaulsky | Kazakhstan | New rail | | | |
| | | | Beyneu–Shalkar | Kazakhstan | New rail | | | |
| | | | Khorgos Dry Port | China, Kazakhstan | Border cost reduction | | | |
| | | | Aktau Port | Kazakhstan | New seaport | | | |
| | 12. | Moscow–Kazan HSR | Moscow–Kazan | Russia | New hicap rail | Proposed | In May 2018, the Eurasian Development Bank committed to financing, signing a cooperation agreement with Russian Railways | 30-May-18 |

**Table B1 :** Silk Road Economic Belt ("Belt")

| Corridor | Nº | Project | Improved Segment | Countries | Improvement type | Status | Details | Status Date |
|---|---|---|---|---|---|---|---|---|
| NEW EURASIAN LAND BRIDGE | 13. | Urumqi–Khorgos Rail | Urumqi–Khorgos | China | New hicap rail | Operational | A new section of railway came into operation between Khorgos and Urumqi. | 30-May-18 |
| | 14. | Urumqi–Khorgos Road | Urumqi–Khorgos | China | New divided road | Operational | Some construction is ongoing. But the road opened and is operational in China and through Kazakhstan to the rest of the inland. | 30-May-18 |
| | 15. | Khorgos–Almaty Road | Khorgos–Almaty | Kazakhstan | New divided road | Operational | | 30-May-18 |
| | 16. | Highway P4/A17 | Astana–Pavlodar | Kazakhstan | Road upgrade | Operational | | 7-Sep-18 |
| | 17. | Highway M36 | Astana–Karaganda | Kazakhstan | Road upgrade | Operational | Currently in use but Kazakhstan is still embarking on other expansions and upgrades for the road. | 7-Sep-18 |
| | 18. | Highway A2 | Almaty–Shymkent Shymkent–Tashkent | Kazakhstan Kazakhstan, Uzbekistan | Road upgrade Road upgrade | Operational | The upgraded road runs from Almaty to a point past Uzynagash. It continues as a two-lane highway to Shymkent. | 11-Oct-18 |
| | 19. | Highway M32 | Shymkent–Tashkent | Kazakhstan, Uzbekistan | Road upgrade | Operational | 11-Oct-18 | |
| CHINA–CENTRAL ASIA–WEST ASIA ECONOMIC CORRIDOR | 20. | Tehran–Mashad Rail | Tehran–Mashhad | Iran, Islamic Rep. | Rail upgrade | Under construction | Electrification project started in 2017 and is projected to be completed in 48 months. | 4-May-18 |
| | 21. | Tehran–Isfahan High Speed Rail | Tehran–Qom–Isfahan | Iran, Islamic Rep. | New hicap rail | Under construction | Expected completion 2021. | 25-Nov-18 |
| | 22. | Kashgar–Tashkent Rail | Kashgar–Andijan | China, Kyrgyz Republic, Uzbekistan | New rail | Proposed | | 19-Feb-18 |
| | 23. | Sher Khan–Herat Rail | Pap–Tashkent Sher Khan–Kunduz–Herat | Uzbekistan Afghanistan | New hicap rail New rail | Under construction | Termiz extension operational since 2012. Expected completion March 2019. | 7-Nov-18 |
| | 24. | Samarkand–Mashhad Rail | Samarkand–Ashgabat–Mashhad | Uzbekistan, Turkmenistan, Iran, Islamic Rep. | Rail upgrade | Operational | | 1-Jun-18 |
| | 25. | Kashgar–Dushanbe Rail | Kashgar–Dushanbe | China, Kyrgyz Republic, Tajikistan | New rail | Proposed | | 1-Sept-17 |
| | 26. | North–South Alternate Road | Jalalabad–Töö Ashuu | Kyrgyz Republic | Road reconstruction | Under construction | | 1-May-18 |
| | 27. | Dushanbe–Afghan Rail | Dushanbe–Kolkhozabad | Tajikistan | Rail upgrade | Proposed | | 23-Aug-18 |
| | 28. | Baku Port Turkmenbashi–Baku | Aktau–Baku | Kazakhstan Turkmenistan | New sea link New sea link | Operational | Baku, Aktau, and Turkmenbashi ports operational. | 5-Jul-18 |
| | 29. | Baku–Tbilisi Rail | Baku–Ganja–Tbilisi | Azerbaijan, Georgia | Rail upgrade | Operational | Launched in October 2017. Though its planning began in 2007, it was postponed several times. | 30-Oct-18 |
| | 30. | Tbilisi–Kars Rail | Tbilisi—Kars | Georgia, Turkey | New rail | Operational | Launched in October 2017. | 28-May-18 |
| | 31. | Anaklia Port Anaklia Anaklia–Istanbul | Anaklia port Georgia Georgia, Turkey | Georgia | New port New hicap rail New sea link | Operational | | 28-Jul-18 |
| | 32. | Ambarli Port | Istanbul | Turkey | New ports and sea links | Operational | | 21-Apr-18 |
| | 33. | Piraeus Port | Athens | Greece | Major port expansion | Operational | | 27-Feb-18 |

**Table B1 :** Silk Road Economic Belt ("Belt")

| Corridor | Nº | Project | Improved Segment | Countries | Improvement type | Status | Details | Status Date |
|---|---|---|---|---|---|---|---|---|
| CHINA–PAKISTAN ECONOMIC CORRIDOR | 34. | Yarkant Road | Tashkurgan–Yarkant (Shache) | China | New road | Proposed | | 25-Jun-17 |
| | 35. | Karakoram Highway | Kashgar–Khunjerab | China | Road reconstruction | Under construction | Reconstruction of China–Pakistan Highway still underway and is expected to be completed by 2019. Highway follows historic trade route. Khunjerab Pass is the only connection between China and Pakistan. Previous upgrades were done outside the scope of the BRI after floods washed out Pakistani roads. | 19-Oct-18 |
| | | Raikot–Shinkiari | Pakistan | New road | | | | |
| | | Shinkiari–Burhan | Pakistan | Road upgrade | | | | |
| | 36. | China–Pakistan Rail | Kashgar–Khunjerab–Taxila | China, Pakistan | New rail | Proposed | Feasibility study planned. | 7-Nov-18 |
| | 37. | Havelian–Hyderabad Capacity Expansion (ML-1) | Havelian–Larkana–Hyderabad | Pakistan | Rail upgrade | Under construction | Upgrade of ML-1 of Pakistan Railways, began in 2018. The project's two phases are expected to be completed by 2021. | 21-Mar-18 |
| | 38. | Karachi–Peshawar Capacity Expansion | Karachi–Hyderabad–Lahore–Peshawar | Pakistan | Rail upgrade | Planning | This railway connects all of Pakistan's major cities and is a transport backbone for the country. | 2-Oct-18 |
| | 39. | Gwadar Rail | Kotla Jam–Quetta–Gwadar | Pakistan | New rail | Planning | The feasibility study has just been completed awaiting approval from China and Pakistan governments. | 2-Apr-18 |
| | 40. | Alternative Gwadar Rail Passage | Gwadar–Karachi | Pakistan | New railroad | Proposed | As of late 2018, no concrete plans, though still mentioned in discussions. | 30-Oct-18 |
| | 41. | Besima–Jacobabad rail | Besima–Jacobabad | Pakistan | New railroad | Planning | In final approval stage. Completion expected 2023. | 27-Mar-18 |
| | 42. | M3/M4 Multan Highway | M2/M3 Bridge–Faisalabad–Multan | Pakistan | New road | Operational | Launched in May 2018 and now in use. | 27-May-18 |
| | 43. | Lahore–Abdul Hakeem Road Upgrade | Lahore–Abdul Hakeem | Pakistan | Road upgrade | Operational | By October 2018, all upgrades were completed, and the highway was ready for opening to traffic. | 9-Nov-18 |
| | 44. | Multan–Sukkur Road | Multan–Sukkur | Pakistan | Road upgrade | Under construction | The first section of the two-way six-lane road was launched in 2018 and is operational. The rest is under construction and to be completed by 2019. | 17-Sep-18 |
| | 45. | Gwadar–Surab Road | Gwadar–Panjgur–Surab | Pakistan | New road | Operational | | 10-Sep-17 |
| | 46. | Surab–DI Khan Road | Surab–Quetta–DI Khan | Pakistan | Road reconstruction | Operational | Launched in 2017 and now in use. | 26-Nov-17 |
| | 47. | M8 Sukkur–Besima Road | Sukkur–Shahdadkot–Besima | Pakistan | New road | Operational | Construction completed in early 2018. | 9-Apr-18 |
| | 48. | Shahdadkot–DI Khan Road | Shahdadkot–DI Khan | Pakistan | New road | Planned | | 25-Nov-18 |
| BANGLADESH–CHINA–INDIA–MYANMAR ECONOMIC CORRIDOR | 49. | Kunming–Calcutta High Speed Rail | Kunming–Mandalay–Chittagong–Dhaka–Calcutta | Bangladesh, China, India, Myanmar | New hicap rail | Proposed | | 13-Sep-18 |
| | 50. | Dali–Lashio Railway | Dali–Ruili–Lashio | China, Myanmar | New rail | Under construction | Under construction since 2011, scheduled for completion in 2021. | 26-Sep-18 |
| | 51. | Kalay–Jiribam Rail | Kalay–Tamu–Jiribam | Myanmar, India | New rail | Under construction | | 18-May-15 |
| | 52. | Dhaka–Bongaon Rail | Dhaka–Bongaon | Bangladesh, India | New rail | Proposed | | 5-Sep-18 |
| | 53. | Kyaukpyu Port | Kyaukpyu–Ann | Myanmar | New rail | Planning | On 8 November 2018, Myanmar and China agreed to scale down the project from US$10 billion to US1.3 billion, from 10 to 2 berths. | 8-Nov-18 |
| | | | Kyaukpyu–Mandalay | Myanmar | Road upgrade | | | |
| | | | Kyaukpyu | Myanmar | New seaport | | | |

**Table B1 :** Silk Road Economic Belt ("Belt")

| Corridor | Nº | Project | Improved Segment | Countries | Improvement type | Status | Details | Status Date |
|---|---|---|---|---|---|---|---|---|
| CHINA–INDOCHINA PENINSULA ECONOMIC CORRIDOR | 54. | Kunming–Vientiane Rail | Kunming–Vientiane | China, Lao PDR | New rail | Under construction | Almost 25 percent of the work done, project to be completed by 2021. Kunming–Hekou rail on China side operational, with wider track boosting cargo capacity. | 22-Jul-18 |
| | 55. | Bangkok–Vientiane Rail | Bangkok–Vientiane | Thailand, Lao PDR | New rail | Under construction | Under construction, with work connecting China with Vietnam, Lao PDR, and Myanmar is expected to be finished by 2021. | 11-Feb-18 |
| | 56. | East Coast Rail Link | Kuala Lumpur–Kota Bharu | Malaysia | New hicap rail | Cancelled or postponed | Construction began in August 2017. On 3 July 2018, Malaysia instructed China Communications Construction to suspend all works. On 12 April 2019, Malaysia indicated work could resume, having negotiated a 1/3 reduction in cost. | 13-Sep-18, 4-Nov-18 12-Apr-19 |
| | 57. | Gemas–Johor Rail Upgrade | Gemas–Johor Bahru | Malaysia | Rail upgrade | Under construction | Malaysia Transport Minister reports that upgrade is 20 percent complete, to be finished in 2022 | 30-Jul-18 |
| | 58. | Bangkok–Kuala Lumpur High | Bangkok–Pedang Besar–Kuala Lumpur | Thailand, Malaysia | Rail upgrade | Proposed Speed Rail | | 7-Nov-18 |
| | 59. | Kuala Lumpur–Singapore High Speed Rail | Kuala Lumpur–Seremban–Singapore | Malaysia, Singapore | New hicap rail | Cancelled or postponed | Officially suspended on 5 September, 2018 at Malaysia's request. Singapore officials report that the construction will resume by 31 May, 2020. | 7-Sep-18 |
| | 60. | Vietnam National High Speed Rail | Hanoi–Ho Chi Minh City | Vietnam | Rail upgrade | Proposed | Planning began in 2007, paused in 2010, now being reconsidered. | 8-Apr-18 |
| | 61 | Vietnam–Cambodia Rail | Phnom Penh–Ho Chi Minh City | Cambodia, Vietnam | New rail | Proposed | Still being discussed, though work on the Bangkok–Phnom Penh rail crossing has commenced. | 15-Feb-18, 28-Jun-18 |
| | 62. | Burma Railway | Nam Tok–Thanbyuzayat | Thailand, Myanmar | New rail | Planned | | 22-Jan-18 |
| | 63. | Sihanoukville Port | Phnom Penh–Sihanoukville | Cambodia | New rail | Under construction | Cambodia's only deep water port. Accompanying special economic zone planned. | 12-Sep-18 |
| | | | Phnom Penh–Sihanoukville | Cambodia | New divided road | | | |
| | | | Sihanoukville | Cambodia | New seaport | | | |
| | 64. | Thai Canal | Satun–Songkhla | Thailand | New sea links | Proposed | Also known as "Kra Canal." Would provide alternative to Strait of Malacca chokepoint. | 6-Apr-18 |
| ADDENDUM: SELECTED RAIL PROJECTS IN AFRICA | 65. | Addis Abeba–Djibouti Railway | Addis Abeba–Djibouti city | Djibouti, Ethiopia | New rail | Operational | Commercial operations began January 2018. To be operated by Chinese firms until 2023 and after that by the Ethio-Djibouti Standard Gauge Rail Transport S.C., a joint venture between Djibouti and Ethiopia. | 19-Nov-18 |
| | 66. | Addis Abeba–Nairobi Railway | Addis Abeba–Nairobi | Ethiopia, Kenya | New rail | Proposed | Kenya–Ethiopia link mentioned among other proposals. No evidence of concrete steps. | 25-Nov-18 |
| | 67. | Juba–Mombasa Railway | Juba–Mombasa | Kenya, South Sudan | New rail | Under construction | | 16-June-18 |

## Table B2 : Maritime Silk Road ("Road")

| Passage | Area | Nº Project | Countries | Type | Status | Details | Status Date |
|---|---|---|---|---|---|---|---|
| CHINA–INDIAN OCEAN–AFRICA–MEDITERRANEAN SEA BLUE ECONOMIC PASSAGE | Indian Ocean (Africa) | 68. Bagamoyo Port | Tanzania | New seaport | Planned | Port approved in 2013, with negotiations still in progress. | 6-Feb-18 |
| | | 69. Dar es Salaam Port | Tanzania | Seaport expansion | Under construction | Improvements for Dar es Salaam port commenced. | 1-Sep-18 |
| | | 70. Lamu Port | Kenya | New seaport | Under construction | In progress. Initiated by Kenya in 2007, completion expected in 2020. | 6-Nov-18 |
| | | 71. Techobanine Port | Mozambique | New seaport | Proposed | | 18-Apr-18 |
| | | 72. Beira Port | Mozambique | Seaport expansion | | Operational | 10-Nov-18 |
| | | 73. Gwadar Port | Pakistan | New seaport | Operational | | 2-Apr-18 |
| | Indian Ocean (Asia) | 74. Duqm Port | Oman | New seaport | Planning | | 4-Jun-18 |
| | | 75. Hambantota Port | Sri Lanka | New seaport | Operational | | 4-Jun-18 |
| | | 76. Colombo Port City | Sri Lanka | New seaport | Under construction | Built on land reclaimed from the Indian Ocean and funded with US$1.4 billion Chinese investment. To be completed in 2020. | 2-Aug-18 |
| | | 77. Kyaukpyu Port | Myanmar | New seaport | Planning | Myanmar and China agreed to scale down the project in 2018 from US$10 billion to US$1.3 billion. With rail link through Myanmar to China, this would present an alternative route to the Strait of Malacca. | 8-Nov-18 |
| | | 78. Melaka Gateway | Malaysia | New seaport | Under construction (stalled) | Port was scheduled for completion in 2019. As of 2018 no construction had been done and regulatory approval has officially lapsed. Future of project is uncertain. | 12-Jul-18 |
| | | 79. Kuala Linggi Port | Malaysia | New seaport | Planned | Minor existing port is in use. | 10-Nov-18 |
| | | 80. Penang Port | Malaysia | New seaport | Operational | | 14-Nov-18 |
| | | 81. Sihanoukville Port | Cambodia | New seaport | Operational | Launched in June of 2018. Accompanied by special economic zone built on Shenzhen model, touted as "next Macao." | 26-Jun-18 |
| | Mediterranean Sea | 82. Suez Economic and Trade Cooperation Zone | Egypt, Arab Rep. | New seaport | Under construction | Located near Suez Canal. | 24-Oct-18 |
| | | 83. Yuzhny Port | Ukraine | New seaport | Operational | | 21-Jan-18 |
| | | 84. Piraeus Port | Greece | New seaport | Operational | | 27-Feb-18 |
| | Atlantic Ocean | 85. Cabinda Port | Angola | New seaport | Under construction | | 25-Jan-17 |
| | | 86. N'Diago Port | Mauritania | New seaport | Under construction | Work in progress on Mauritania's largest sea port, located near Senegal border. | 13-Dec-17 |
| | | 87. Tema Port | Ghana | New seaport | Operational | In use but some civil works are still ongoing. | 14-Oct-18 |
| | Pacific Ocean | 88. Thai canal | Thailand | New sea links | Proposed | | 6-Apr-18 |
| | | 89. Kuantan Port | Malaysia | New seaport | Operational | | 4-Nov-18 |
| CHINA–OCEANIA–SOUTH PACIFIC BLUE ECONOMIC PASSAGE | Pacific Ocean | — (none proposed) | — | — | — | — | — |
| | Indian Ocean | 90. Darwin Port | Australia | Seaport expansion | Operational | | 17-Jun-18 |